I0824693

DREAM FACADES

DREAM FACADES

The Cruel Architecture of Reality TV

JACK BALDERRAMA MORLEY

Astra House New York

Astra House
A Division of Astra Publishing House
astrahouse.com

Printed in the United States of America

Library of Congress Cataloging-in-Publication Data is available upon request.
ISBN: 978-1-6626-0292-4

First edition
10 9 8 7 6 5 4 3 2 1

Design by Alissa Theodor
The text is set in Warnock Pro light.
The titles are set in Helvetica Neue LT Pro.

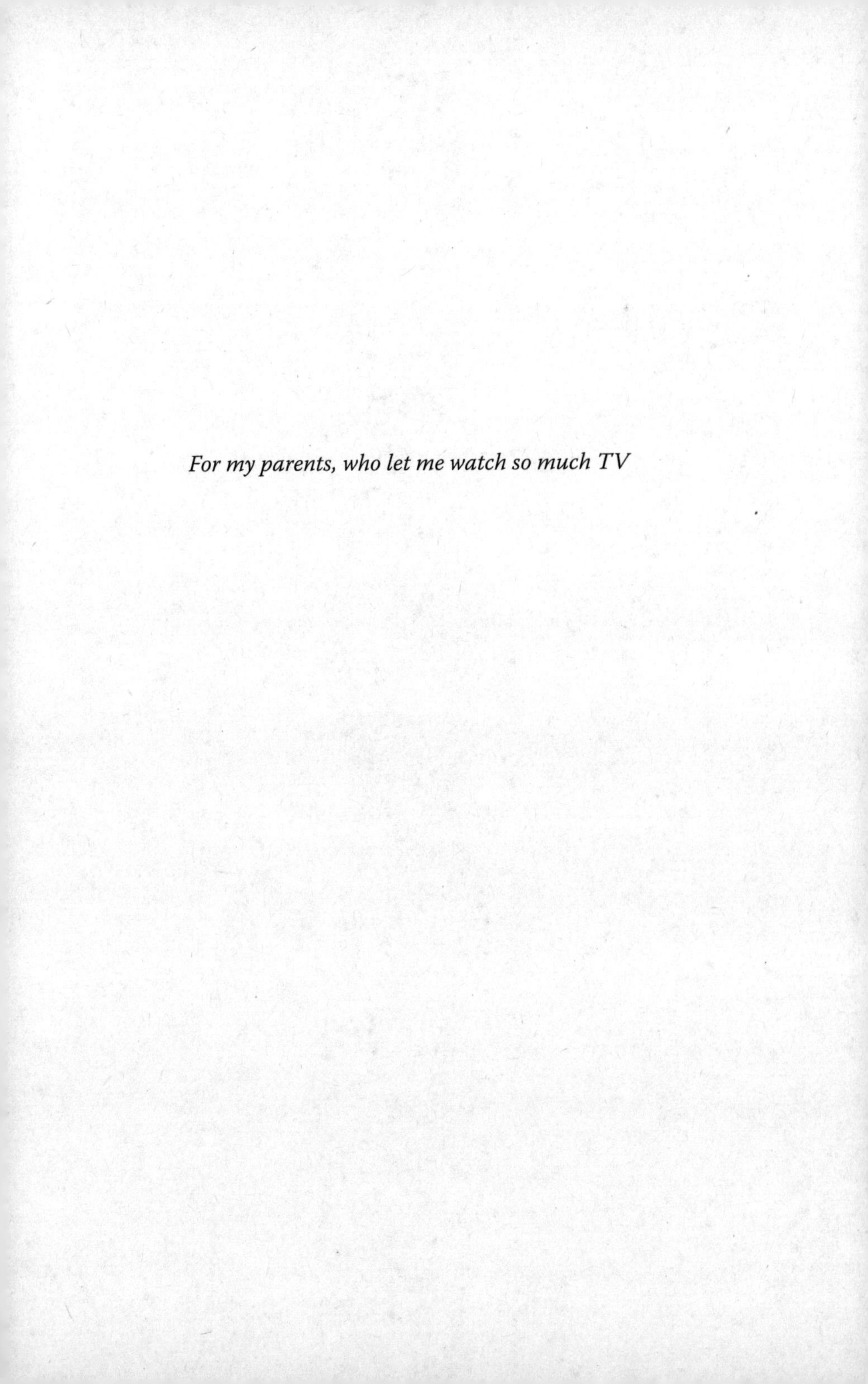

For my parents, who let me watch so much TV

When I was young, I saw something that changed my life: a twenty-something woman and her best friend moving into a condo complex supposedly in West Hollywood, California. Lauren Conrad and Heidi Montag were starting a glossy new life together in the Hillside Villas, a Spanish Colonial Revival–style development. Conrad and Montag would meet a new friend by the pool, bring boyfriends home, and celebrate after landing jobs in creative industries, Montag in PR and Conrad at *Teen Vogue.* Conrad would leave in her BMW convertible to spend a seemingly unending amount of money brunching at various restaurants and partying at celebrity hot spot Les Deux. At the end of the first season, she would temporarily move with her boyfriend into a Malibu beach house with a wall of windows overlooking the Pacific. This, I thought from my parents' couch in frigid Poughkeepsie, New York, was real living. This, I thought, was just what I needed. This was *The Hills.*

In retrospect, what I really needed was SSRIs and a broader worldview, but I was years away from both. So sitting there, stuffing my face with DOTS, my candy of choice, I decided: Los Angeles! If I could move to Los Angeles after graduation, life would really begin. The glittering life on-screen felt more real than the gray one around me. MTV's hit had sucked me in.

I did move to LA, but my life didn't turn out exactly like it had for the ladies on-screen. For better or worse, I'm not a wealthy white woman from Laguna Beach, my beat-up Honda Civic was no BMW, and my apartment did not have an ocean view. Real life wasn't like reality TV, it turned out. Unlike Conrad and company, I didn't find a glittering life in California, and after a couple of years, I left.

But I wasn't so easily robbed of my naivety. Over the years, I've fallen for plenty of other reality TV homes: I nursed heartbreak alongside Shereé Whitfield while she built her chateau on *The Real Housewives of Atlanta*, felt some sense of superiority leering at the glossy *Selling Sunset* mansions during the first savvy-villain-supreme Trump presidency, and found what felt like friends amid the laughter and tears of the *Love Island* villa during pandemic lockdowns.

As I've gotten older, and more doors of possibility have shut, and friends have moved away or hunkered down with partners in safe little homes, I have found not just solace in reality TV homes but surrogate relationships, celebrations, and dreams fulfilled. While my rent has gone up and roaches have found their way onto my warping floors, reality TV homes have not deteriorated—on the contrary, they get more fantastic every season.

Homes have been central to reality TV since it began. The genre's juggernauts revolve around residential design. The Bachelor has his mansion, Chip and Joanna Gaines their modern farmhouses, *Love Is Blind* its weird little condos. Each of these homes offers something different, but they have a lot in common. Reality TV, ironically, is all about fantasy—visions of love, wealth, and victory projected into beautiful beach houses where, at least for a few minutes, audiences can repose. Even when the homes on-screen are squalid *Hoarders* huts, the promise of salvation from a *Queer Eye* is always waiting in the wings.

Times are bad, but life on-screen is good. Reality homes offer windows into the good life at a time when the good life is increasingly out of reach. They provide viewers of all stripes relatively guiltless ways of enjoying some of the most conservative fantasies in American culture: getting ahead, getting married, and getting a house in the Hills, or at least dating a guy with a Malibu beach house for the summer. The rest of the world will fend for itself. Loneliness is an epidemic, cities are burning, and people find inspiration in Kim Kardashian declaring "calmness is my superpower" and swanning around her home decorated in soporific neutrals for an hour every week. What a gift to be able to tune in.

But these homes offer more than just a taste of happiness or escape; instead they seem to be invading our world, overwhelming our day-to-day sense of reality in our lovely hovels. Life in the United States in the twenty-first century feels increasingly unreal, and these shows have offered me and millions of others reassuring feelings of reality. That's part of reality TV's core offering—if it feels fake, it fails. Even though audiences intellectually know that the situations on display are engineered by producers lingering off-camera, something about the shows—a contestant's reaction to winning a competition, a spark between two new lovers, the home a House Hunter chooses—must *feel* real. It's this feeling of reality that keeps people like me coming back as our relationships fall apart and our jobs disappear and our world ping-pongs between fresh hells every news cycle.

The relationship between reality TV and our physical homes makes the feeling of reality these shows provide so powerful. Reality TV is an unusual form of entertainment for a lot of reasons, but among the most important is that it was one of the first forms of media to create home-to-home visual connections. Radio was the first mass medium to beam live information to an audience at home; reality TV develops that relationship further, wiring visions of real living rooms into our own. Our homes are critical providers of our own sense of reality, and reality TV expands and warps that sense, letting the ancient forces shaping our homes evolve with digital media, like viruses given new hosts.

These homes are more than stage sets for drama; they're real places swollen with the fantasies projected onto them. These are lurid houses of intrigue and deception, haunted mansions twisted by disillusionment with modern life and its supposed rewards: dream facades for a new reality. And our homes have changed, too, with these dream facades sutured onto them, turning into physical-digital hybrid homes that wrap us in fun-house horrors.

It's not a great situation. And it doesn't seem to be headed in a great direction.

Despite the historically unprecedented wealth and power of the United States, a lot of the people in this country, maybe even most, don't feel good, and the path to a lasting euphoria seems gone. As every aspect of life is privatized and turned into a product to be sold to you, even just the feeling of being real has become a luxury. People venture down many avenues in their quest to feel more real—they work hard, they fall in love, they buy property. These avenues are roads to nowhere, exhausting us while we chase the things that have been advertised as the things that define a life. In our hybrid homes, these avenues intertwine, creating a map of how messed up life in this country is right now.

If we don't figure out where we're going, we're going to be stuck in isolated homes in soulless apartment buildings or subdivisions, sitting on our couches watching rich people bicker while the world melts around us, wasting our last minutes wishing we were white ladies in Malibu dating boys with names like Justin Bobby who don't treat us very well. But we don't need to be constantly jostled into competitive isolation or rely on surrogate homes to fulfill our dreams. I don't want that. I don't think most people do. Most of us, I think, live in a world we would deem at least a little subpar, one we wouldn't choose if we had another option.

Where did we go wrong?

Americans have a lot of psychological baggage about their homes that needs to be unpacked before things can get any better. There is a kind of cruel optimism, as the literary theorist Lauren Berlant might have put it, in Americans' relationships with their homes, a faith that settling down and buying a place with some nice light and room for the kids might be the start of a happy new life, a chance at transformation. And then the same old world rolls out around you. Our homes isolate us, destroy communities, and erase histories on stolen land, emptying us out while renting back to us little feelings that promise to make us whole. Americans live in cruel homes.

This book proposes that this is not the way things need to be. By diving deep into these shows and the homes that appear in them, we can find a different path forward. The rest, as Natasha Bedingfield sings in the intro to *The Hills*, is still unwritten.

Reality is just an illusion

I saw the best minds of my generation enthralled by drone shots of glass walls sliding open to infinity pools that fell into the canyons above Los Angeles.

That's the power of *Selling Sunset*, the hit reality show on Netflix in which real estate agents at the Oppenheim Group sell homes and get in fights about who is mean and who is nice while wearing impractical outfits and saying things such as, "Luxury, glamour, style is my thing." It's a mostly white, patriarchal wonderland overseen by the muscled Oppenheim brothers, a world where wealth is triumphal and success comes in the form of sales, a kind of Southern California Gordon Gekko fantasy set to a pounding pop soundtrack, and it offers a big, glistening window into how homes on-screen can distort our feelings of reality at home.

The *Selling Sunset* environment is not a setting I'd normally seek out, for a variety of reasons, but something about watching those giant glass walls slide open produces pleasure that I can't refuse. For a significant portion of the pandemic, I was curled up on my couch watching this show, and I wasn't the only one. Plenty of people whose critical thinking I admire sat enraptured by a program driven by heterosexuality and capitalism. One season culminated in an episode in which an agent—on her wedding day—sold the house where she was getting married. Her friends' general reaction was, "That's awesome," a slam dunk for the Protestant work ethic. I would probably feel my soul leave my body if I had to endure that day in real life, but seeing it onscreen, I was transfixed and maybe even teared up.

What's happening here?

Yes, I'm a lifelong fan of reality TV, but more than once I've caught a reflection of myself in my screen after another episode of *Selling Sunset* fades to black and wondered why watching this show is what I'm doing with my one wild and precious life. What's the source of its power? It's not ambient TV, meant to play in the background while you do chores or whatever else—it's too gripping, weirdly enough, even though it's half advertisements for homes most of us will never be able to afford. It's not purely real estate porn, either, judging from the characters' popularity online. If it's escapism, it's an odd form of it; a lot of the show depicts office work and company politicking, which I get enough of in real life. And we see people living in these homes only when one of the realtors consummates her rags-to-riches storyline by moving into one. *Lifestyles of the Rich and Famous* this is not. It's not even *MTV Cribs*. It's hard to identify exactly what it is.

"Reality is just an illusion," Christine Quinn, *Selling Sunset*'s original villain and Cassandra of our times, said on the *Call Her Daddy* podcast, one of her many media appearances since the show turned her into a celebrity of sorts. Fans ate up the realtor turned Balenciaga model's sassy confidence and the way she evaded her castmates' earnest outrage over her supposed transgressions by twisting the truth and rolling her eyes at the lame finger-wagging of the morality police around her.

In this exchange, Mary Bonnet, the virtuous new wife mentioned above, confronted Quinn about something uncouth the latter had said:

Quinn: It was a joke.

Bonnet: It's not a joke—stop joking, because your jokes aren't funny.

Quinn: My jokes are hilarious.

Bonnet: No, they're not.

Quinn: Yes, they are.

Bonnet: Then why does everybody have a problem with you?

Quinn: Because they have no sense of humor! What can I say?

Bonnet: Or you're acting like a bitch.

Quinn: Okay, maybe I am.

Like the show, Quinn was impossible to pin down. (In interviews, she claimed that the show's editors made her look worse than she was in person—she left the show after its fifth season.) She was delighted when one castmate called her look a combination of Elizabeth Holmes and Ivanka Trump, and, well, of course she was. The slickly disorienting, opulent show upholding conservative consumerist values was the perfect product of the original Trump years. And like the wave of right-wing populism that washed over the country in 2016, *Selling Sunset*'s aesthetics had been brewing for some time.

Adam DiVello pioneered a new style in the aughts with *Laguna Beach* and my lodestar, *The Hills*, which featured a still camera, cinematic look and feel that was a world away from the gonzo documentary style of *Survivor* and other Y2K reality juggernauts. And DiVello's influence grows, reshaping the *Real Housewives* franchise and even the Kardashians' Hulu show, which has adopted some of his signature glossy stillness. DiVello made life on reality TV look seductive and aspirational, partly by taking some of the realistic unpredictability out of it; *The Hills's* finale ended with a teary goodbye between Kristin Cavallari and her supposed on-again-off-again boyfriend, caught with a crane shot that pulled back to reveal a stage lot, a fake Hollywood sign background, and a crowd of producers choreographing the scene.

In worlds like these, it's hard to know what to hold on to. On *Selling Sunset*, the houses are the constant, the medium in which all else exists, the stages for the fights and speeches, the slurred insults, the stormy exits. The homes are more than backdrops; they're the reasons for the seasons, the goods that must be bought and sold to keep this economy running, what gives this universe its form. The spell cast by the show can be understood only by piecing together the puzzle of its homes.

If you've seen the show, the classic *Selling Sunset* home springs to mind without description. There's some variety, but the canonical homes mimic each other as though they all grew from the same root buried in the Hollywood Hills. If you haven't had the pleasure of watching this series, picture big, modern, white homes featuring an aesthetic so polished and consistent that they sometimes have an uncanny valley effect, as though someone typed "modernist building" into an AI image generator and built the results. The slickness melds beautifully with DiVello's cinematic approach. White walls neatly frame confrontations;

views of Los Angeles fading into the distance make the perfect backdrops for staged dramas.

The house at 8408 Hillside Avenue, featured heavily in season 1, when it was under construction, and whose completion was revealed at the start of season 2, is the exemplar. It's a five-bedroom, 20,000-square-foot stunner on a promontory overlooking the Sunset Strip that sold for $35.5 million.

Jason Oppenheim, president and founder of the Oppenheim Group, seems to nod in recognition when I asked him about it. "Hard to beat that house, because it is the highest quality and best designed and curated house arguably in all of the Hollywood Hills," he tells me. The Hillside house's details are so minimal that the building looks like a digital rendering. Ceilings are high and interiors are cavernous. Walls are white, stairs float, guardrails are thin slabs of cantilevered glass, and of course, glass walls slide back before an infinity pool that seems to melt into the horizon.

The house sets the tone for others that follow. Jason and others confirmed that what you see on the show reflects what's popular in the area. On the show, the agent Chelsea Lazkani calls the aesthetic a "sexy MoMA" look, referencing the massive and modern New York museum, and she's not wrong. There's something cold and self-important—magisterial—about the vibe, a sort of chilly American imperial feel. It was designed by South African architecture firm SAOTA, creators of superluxe homes around the world. Mark Bullivant, a principal there, tells me that the aesthetic has roots in the Hills; the area's midcentury-modern Case Study Houses partially inspired 8408 Hillside.

"Hillside is kind of one canyon across from the Stahl House, which is obviously an iconic structure," Bullivant tells me. The Stahl House is one of the mid-twentieth-century Case Study Houses sponsored by *Arts and Architecture* magazine, designed by California architect Pierre Koenig. The Case Study Houses set the standard for progressive postwar home design in the United States, and photos sold a vision of modern architecture that was almost supernaturally elegant and serene. "Taking a stroll along Sunset Boulevard and seeing how that Stahl House roof just hovers over you—that certainly had quite a big impact in the way that we have thought about these hillside homes," Bullivant says.

The midcentury aesthetic comes up regularly on the show. Houses by midcentury Southern California design luminaries Richard Neutra and Harry Gesner make appearances. (Gesner is one of Jason's favorite architects, he tells me.) But at first blush, comparing the design of bombastic homes such as 8408 Hillside to Koenig's or Neutra's elegant midcentury creations seems like a stretch. Midcentury modernism has been glamorized by magazines such as *Dwell* and hypebeasty trendhunters as the style of choice for sensitive aesthetes, an alternative to the nostalgia-driven traditional styles typical of suburbia. Midcentury modernism is progressive and forward-thinking while still being warm and down-to-earth, not loftily floating above like these aloof manses. But over the past decade or so, a handful of academics have published books complicating this take on the style.

In *Little White Houses: How the Postwar Home Constructed Race in America*, historian Dianne Suzette Harris argues that American modernism in the 1950s was the style of elites. In 1949, Russell Lynes, an editor at *Harper's Magazine*, published his famous tongue-in-cheek "brow chart," which divided forms of entertainment and decor not by class, as nineteenth-century tastemakers might have done, but by "brow height." Lowbrow tastes tended toward beer and overstuffed chairs, upper-middlebrow to Empire-style furniture and dry martinis. A simple red wine and furniture designed by midcentury modernists Charles and Ray Eames and Kurt Versen were for those in the know at the top.

Harris also describes how Elizabeth Gordon, editor of *House Beautiful*, one of the premier home-design magazines of the postwar period, espoused the style we now call midcentury modernism as a gentler alternative to the often harsher styles of prewar Europe. She had more than an aesthetic agenda. Gordon disliked European modernism's ties to dangerous ideologies such as communism or other kinds of continental radicalism. Gordon celebrated the softened American form of modernism that rounded off some sharp edges and had no ties to scary political systems. She enjoyed an American form of home design in the service of the American political and economic system.

The America that Gordon celebrated was, to put it lightly, a mixed bag. It was a triumphant nation emerging victorious from two world wars to an unprecedented economic boom, but it was also deeply racist, still legally segregated, and actively trying to erase Native American culture. Those years were the country's halcyon days for white supremacy, and these midcentury modern homes were by and large only available to white people.

Kristina Wilson, an art historian and author of *Mid-Century Modernism and the American Body: Race, Gender, and the Politics of Power in Design*, thinks nostalgia for the modernist architecture of the '50s is not easily separated from that political past. She tells me about a parallel she sees between midcentury modernism and American Colonial Revival home styles, which were extremely popular in the late nineteenth and early twentieth centuries and still are today. Colonial Revival homes feature horizontal siding, often white, shutters, and a chimney—a quintessential suburban look. One hundred years ago, Colonial Revival styles were simple, nostalgic alternatives to florid Victorian trends, with their curlicues and turrets and fairy-tale decoration, just as midcentury modernism was a palette cleanser after the gaudy 1980s and the McMansion kitsch of the 1990s.

"In short," Wilson tells me, "midcentury modernism is today's Colonial Revival."

It's an unsettling notion, especially to a *Dwell* editor like me, but the parallels between midcentury modernism and the *Selling Sunset* style are becoming more apparent. The show is something of a white supremacist fever dream in which idealized white bodies pursue marriage, reproduction, and the accumulation of wealth. The main cast in the first season is all white; some non-white buyers and agents appear as the show goes on, but whiteness is the inescapable norm. Being Mexican American and having spent two years living in LA and rolling my eyes at Anglos telling me where to get the best tacos in the city, I'm made a little sheepish by my self-betrayal. Sorry to the ancestors: I've been lining colonizer pockets while curled up on my couch and calling it self-care.

Maybe, I tell myself, eager to salvage some self-respect, there's hope for these *Selling Sunset* homes. After all, they're not midcentury-modern revival—they're sleeker, bigger, brighter. It's tempting to think that these homes might've shed some social baggage in the same way they ditched the wall-to-wall carpeting and avocado-colored appliances. But sadly, though their details might've changed, these houses resurrect the '50s playbook in their relationship to their city.

The post–World War II period was a time of white migration from cities to suburbs, when the perception of danger downtown drove white families to areas such as the Hollywood Hills. When I talk to Aaron Johnson, a developer whose property was featured in the second season, I hear a refrain that sounds straight out of the Eisenhower era. "LA is just a mess," he says. "It's heartbreaking to see what's happening. . . . Politics in general, the homeless, the crime. It's horrific . . . LA in general is just kinda breaking down."

Never mind that the realities of crime are often far from what's screamed in today's politically motivated headlines. People head to the Hills to get away from the scary threats of city living. When the realtors on the show talk about the *Selling Sunset* homes, none of them are desirable because they're in walkable neighborhoods buzzing with life. These houses are as disconnected as possible. Their only connection to the wider world is via views of the city. Those views aren't a physical part of the homes, but they might as well be: They're a defining part of the *Selling Sunset* style, and they, too, have roots in midcentury modernism. The photographer Julius Shulman took iconic photos of the Case Study Houses and one of his most famous is of the Stahl House, with two white women lounging with the city spread out below them. The views are scenic and beautiful, sure, but they're more than that.

"Views . . . are all about power," Wilson tells me, "power of sight over others, the power of being removed and being able to look down and assert control through visual knowledge of the entire so-called playing board of the game of life."

Doug Fregolle, a homeowner I talked to whose house was featured on the show, tells me something similar: "You live in the Hollywood Hills with a view, you have made it."

"Every design decision for a house in the Hills is all to boost your ego, and that's why it caters to the rich bachelors," Jhoiey Ramirez, a designer who worked on several homes on the show, tells me. "Their ego feeds their success, and their success feeds their ego. Their home needs to keep feeding both."

—

So views are all about power—but they don't provide people with actual power to control what they see, just the feeling of being powerful. What is actual power today?

"The prime technique of power is now escape, slippage, elision, and avoidance," wrote the Polish sociologist Zygmunt Bauman in 1999. He described the era as one in which the old, ossified power structures of nineteenth-century Europe had been melted down, but instead of being replaced by the new, solid, idealist societies that radicals envisioned, society stayed melted, perpetually unstable. In this "liquid" world, the powerful no longer sit on thrones in castles, their names emblazoned across the land, but instead are constantly flying across borders, hidden behind layers of shell companies, always able to avoid answering to the people they control. Because the pace of change is now so fast and unpredictable, it's nearly impossible for people to organize and agitate for better conditions, and so most people spend their lives in a whirlpool, just trying to keep their heads above the water.

The sociologist wrote about the architecture of the liquid modern world, but he focused on contemporary gathering places such as airports and shopping malls. He didn't write about homes in the Hollywood Hills, and he never got the chance to watch *Selling Sunset*. But the interiors of these homes sometimes feel more like airports or malls than like traditional houses, and Bauman was so adept at analyzing the relationship between power and culture in the weird internet age that his commentary feels just as relevant to the show.

"Powerful, 'more real than reality' images on ubiquitous screens set the standard for reality and its evaluation, as well as for the urge to make the 'lived' reality more palatable," he wrote about TV. Bauman understood how the wealthy would sneak off to private hideaways where they wouldn't be disturbed by their subjects. I think he also would've understood why these houses look the way they do. Though they follow the '50s playbook in their relationship to LA, the architecture of the *Selling Sunset* homes is a sort of Pokemon-evolved form of postwar design, adapted to the delirious, digital capitalist world of twenty-first-century America.

The homes' interiors are slick and expansive. Gone are woods and natural textures that could snag the eye, replaced by expanses of glossy

Sheetrock. Details are minimized so one's ego can float unfettered, and infinity pools provide the illusion that these spaces go on forever, that the entire universe is set dressing to your living room. It's a frictionless aesthetic of boundless personal freedom, private isolation, and power over others.

Ironically, the same trappings of modernism that gratify owners' egos lend a veneer of progressivism to these homes and their residents. If the houses were traditional, they would signal that their owners were holdovers from the past, aging monarchs clinging to their beloved brickwork. These are homes for people who want to separate themselves from the nostalgic set living in dated traditional homes and feel forward-thinking, market-savvy: real estate flippers, the founder of the app known as Uber for dogs. This is progressive modernism for people for whom progress means crypto, Teslas, and the unfettered flow of capital, not the liberation of working people or some other utopian end.

"As in the past, we are motivated by an eminently modern impulse to transgress," Bauman writes, "but we are no longer amused by, or even tempted to imagine, its goal or destination."

These houses—and these people—aren't just in the Hollywood Hills. They seem to be everywhere wealth accumulates, from the penthouses of New York City to the hillsides of South Africa. They're glistening bastions of security and control, offering the feeling of being one step ahead in a turbulent world where the seasons change ever more extremely and the ground is in constant danger of sliding away.

If Elizabeth Gordon of *House Beautiful* saw midcentury modernism as embodying postwar American values, then this modernism reflects twenty-first-century global capitalist values. It's architecture that says, "Oh, no, I'm not like those old traditionalist fat cats. My desires are new. I'm modern. I'm something better." This contradiction between the aesthetics of dynamism and the attempt to consolidate power and status in stable form is, I think, what makes these homes feel so odd. There's an anxiety about them.

In the liquid modern world, "the search for identity is the ongoing struggle to arrest or slow down the flow," Bauman writes. People want to "make it" in life. What they want to make is a stable, coherent self, their own pocket of enduring order in a constantly changing world, even though that may never be possible.

The owners of these homes have learned how to thrive in liquidity, so they don't want their homes to evoke the solidity of yesteryear, but they still crave a reassuring stability. They want to shellac the liquid world, give it a thin veneer of solidity. If liquid modernism is the glossy, placeless feel of airport terminals and oversize art repositories, then shellacked modernism is the draping of that stylistic language of efficiency and wealth over spaces that are meant to provide a sense of comfort and home. Trying to create a sense of belonging with an aesthetic of placelessness gives these homes their uncanny tension.

Bauman had some thoughts about those brow distinctions that Russell Lynes wrote about. In liquid modernity, the sociologist thought, signifiers of taste were no longer so neatly segregated.

"The sign of belonging to a cultural elite today is maximum tolerance and minimal choosiness," he writes in *Culture in a Liquid Modern World*. "Cultural snobbery consists of an ostentatious denial of snobbery."

The new elite no longer defines itself solely by taking in the ballet and ignoring the hoi polloi. Now the elite watch reality TV in addition to reading Polish sociology, reveling in their ability to navigate every current of the liquid world.

The creators of *Selling Sunset,* I think, know this on some level, and the show regularly includes segments that are seemingly mostly set up to make the people on the show seem stupid or inept, as though to appeal to a sense of superiority among the tastemakers in the audience. We get to laugh at agents fumbling while trying to plug in a light or misquoting American pop culture idioms ("The silent of the lamb"). We get to look down on the homes and marvel at how huge and tacky they are compared to our distinguished tastes. *I* would never live there, we say to ourselves, tucked away in our ramshackle cocoons, savoring the feeling that although we don't have stable health insurance and may never pay off our student loans, we are still somehow better off than the people on the show. Watching the show, we get to relax and pretend the world isn't melting, war isn't raging, we're not living in a country on colonized land. What a delight. How fun.

Selling Sunset does more than offer its ramshackle-dwelling audience glossy skyline views that only the rich can otherwise afford. The show and its houses distort our feelings about the world and our place in it, making our homes feel fundamentally different than they otherwise would.

In 2017, Tarisai Ngangura wrote in *Vice* about the appeal of *Laguna Beach*, DiVello's first reality TV show, which premiered in 2004 while the United States was occupying Iraq and just a few months after the Abu Ghraib photos were published: "Why think about human rights abuses when you can spend your hours deciphering if Lauren Conrad really was a natural blonde?" The show is not just a temporary escape from reality—it reframes reality, turning it into something light and feathery, taking away the weight of Americans' responsibility for our country's atrocities, letting us float freely over the horizon into the big, beautiful California sky.

Shellacked entertainment lets me forget that my job is perpetually unstable, that my rent could spike at the end of the month, that a shooter could storm into the few public spaces I still enjoy and massacre me and everyone around. Isn't it nice of our entertainment overlords to give us just a taste of what it must feel like to be in control?

Views transform the homes on *Selling Sunset* into magisterial thrones, and the show makes us feel like it's doing something similar to our own living rooms, however dumpy. That's what makes this kind of entertainment so insidious. It gives a false sense of accomplishment, as though just by watching it and looking down on the vain and shallow people and houses on our screens, we are engaging politically, even though we're not doing anything to improve conditions for ourselves or others. It's pseudo escapism that makes us feel like there's nothing we need to escape from because it reinforces a sense that we are safe at the top of the ladder by virtue of our aesthetic tastes. And so our potential wastes away on a Wayfair couch.

If, perhaps, it all seems too bleak, I think there's hope. All those magisterial vistas and sliding glass doors so frequently repeated feel formulaic. *Selling Sunset*, at least to me, got a little boring. The homes have changed, no longer so slick and white, though they're still modernist monsters overlooking the city. Quinn's gone. It's only a matter of time before the show runs its course, as they all do. We'll wave farewell to our gaggle of marriage-obsessed realtors, and something new will capture our attention. There are already spin-offs and copycats to glom on to. But I'm trying to hold on to that feeling of being bored rather than sliding into the next in pursuit of some new distracting high.

If shellacked modernity becomes boring enough, it can lead its audience to ask for something different. It might let us realize that we should demand more from our screens, from ourselves. Our desire for—and arguably, need for—a little mindless entertainment are unlikely to go away, and there are certainly ways to improve shows like *Selling Sunset*, including diversifying the cast, which DiVello and his team have done over the seasons. There was even an all-Black spin-off, *Selling Tampa*, though that was canceled after just one season. But we may be walking toward better options when we should be running. What's the alternative? Reality can't stay frozen forever. The liquid modern world is swirling beneath us, ready to collapse at any moment like a California landslide, burying us in the mud we try so hard to ignore. Our future may depend on us redirecting our attention to the watery depths yawning under our own feet.

Selling Sunset is just one example of the many ways that hybrid homes are playing us. DiVello may have polished a certain effect of reality TV, but the genre has been distorting viewers' sense of self since it began.

People who are very different than myself

Hybrid homes are as old as reality TV, but those origins are hard to pinpoint because the genre is hard to define. No ancients ever set definitions for reality TV as they did for drama or tragedy. It's a know-it-when-you-see-it thing that resists a simple definition. Was Julia Child's public-channel cooking show reality TV? How about *Soul Train*, with its amateur dancers? Or the hours of unscripted sports content that run on ESPN? And what about C-SPAN's live video feed, which isn't so different from the live streams from the *Big Brother* house?

By some definitions, reality TV is as old as broadcast programming. Arguably the first reality TV show, *Candid Camera*, premiered in 1948 on ABC, the same year the network launched, and a form of it started even earlier as a radio show. The prank show set up little ruses in public and used cameras to watch while ordinary people were bamboozled. Producers relabeled a closet in a theater lobby as a restroom and watched while confused visitors stumbled out; girls were tricked into thinking a hunk was going to be their new teacher, and cameras recorded their blissful reaction.

The show was a hit and stayed on the air in one form or another for decades, finally ending in 2014. *Candid Camera* was a sort-of first reality show, but for most of its run there weren't enough similar shows on air to create a recognizable genre. And although the show pioneered the concept of recording non-actors going about their lives, it lacked certain hallmarks of modern reality TV, such as a cast of recurring personalities.

That changed with the next program that some consider to be the first reality show: *An American Family*, which premiered in 1973. During its only season, it followed the Loud family of Santa Barbara, California. The Louds were an upper-middle-class white nuclear family, and cameras recorded them for several months, during which the parents separated. The show was a sensation and elicited the kind of critical panic that hit reality shows would in the future: Did these attention-hungry Californians really represent America? What did their popularity have to say about the country's moral decline? But still a cohesive genre failed to materialize around the show, and by today's standards it doesn't feel like reality TV. *An American Family*, which ran on PBS, had lots of long, rambling scenes and some poignant ones, particularly based around one of the sons, Lance, who was a young gay guy living in Andy Warhol's New York, trying to figure out how to relate to his square parents back home. Documentarian Craig Gilbert shot the show with a sort of cinema verité style unlike what we'd recognize as reality TV now. *An American Family* did, however, inspire the next breakthrough show, which was definitively of the genre.

Seven strangers walked into a loft in 1992 at the invitation of soap opera producer Mary-Ellis Bunim and documentarian Jonathan Murray. Their new show on MTV developed hallmarks of reality TV: gathering a group of strangers to live in a house together, to-camera "confessionals," a cast trip. Everything about the living situation was constructed. Privacy was minimal; a dearth of doors allowed cameras to glide about. Soap opera and documentary blended, edited to move at the pace of music videos, to create something new. The show was of the moment, a novel kind of entertainment for a network focused on the young, and it changed TV for decades to follow, not only by turning entertainers on-screen into surrogate friends but also by encouraging audiences to turn themselves into televisual stars.

When I was a bored kid, passing the time by staring at the wall in exurban sprawl before Lauren Conrad was a twinkle in a producer's eye, *The Real World* opened a window. It showed me groups of friends living in sprawling homes in big cities, where people were creative and expressive and didn't have homework or office jobs or any responsibilities other than being themselves, having fun, and getting naked in hot tubs. Danny Roberts making out with his military boyfriend on the New Orleans edition was something of a sexual awakening for me. The entire Las Vegas series, which should have come with a free STI test, was another. The show promised that suburban isolation was illusory, that somewhere out there, waiting, was something more sensual, more real.

For better or worse, the show did portend things to come, but it didn't presage a wonderland where people don't have to work and can just be themselves. Instead, being yourself has become one of the many jobs you might have, and the better you are at marketing your identity on Instagram or Tinder or LinkedIn or wherever else, the better chance you have of "success." The whole world is now that magic mansion, and we're all a bunch of strangers constantly performing our identities for a languishing audience.

If reality TV started with *The Real World*, then the first reality TV home was in New York City's SoHo neighborhood, where the premier season was shot in 1992. The fortunes of that area are important for the history of the genre. Hybrid homes aren't just the result of digital media infiltrating the physical world—digital media have evolved from the physical world, built on brick-and-mortar bases that have embodied cultural neuroses for millennia.

But instead of going back that far, we can turn to SoHo's more recent evolution. In the 1990s, the area was on its way to becoming the luxury jungle it is now, but the building that hosted the first season of *The Real World*, 565 Broadway, was at its best when it opened in 1860. It was something of a big deal. An article in *Frank Leslie's Illustrated Newspaper*, then a major outlet, hailed its completion: "In proportion, in chasteness of design, in rich and elegant finish, and in perfect keeping, we know no building in the whole length of Broadway that can equal it." A full-page illustration showed men in top hats and women in gowns peering into its windows, each made of a single pane of heavy plate glass, supposedly the largest ever made, the article says—the ancestors of those massive *Selling Sunset* sliders.

The luxurious outside was matched by its interior. Architect John Kellum designed 565 Broadway's cast-iron structure with a marble palazzo-style facade, evocative of Italian merchant mansions, for Ball, Black & Co, a luxury retailer and manufacturer. The ground floor was for selling gems, watches, and silverware, the *Frank Leslie's* article reported before claiming that it didn't have the space to adequately cover the dazzling and elaborate decor. On the second floor, where the roommates would one day make their home, were European paintings, plus "a wilderness of rich clocks, bronzes, marble statuary, and splendid mantel ornaments of every kind." The third floor was for lighting fixtures, and on the level above, more than two hundred workers produced many of the goods for sale below—a common setup at the time.

But all that luster didn't last. In the ensuing decades, prime shopping districts migrated uptown, and less luxurious retailers and manufacturers moved in. Later in the 20th century, New York's overall industrial economy declined; manufacturing moved out of the city to cheaper places in the American South and Southwest as well as overseas, and SoHo's buildings started to empty. The once glorious district dimmed.

Now, 565 Broadway is still nice, and a renovation wrapped up in 2025 that restored the marble facade, but it's not necessarily a building you would notice as you walked by. There's a Madewell on the ground floor, and the building blends in with the high-end chain-store strip mall that runs down Broadway. The area is now packed with tourists and influencers, once again a center of the consumer universe.

There's a rosy image of how artists brought SoHo back to life after its decline: Scrappy creatives rehabilitated ruins, turned them into homes. Midcentury mavericks such as Donald Judd blossomed amid the grit and birthed a new American art style that forsook illusory image-making and embraced physical "reality" manifested in plywood and steel boxes—minimalism, fuck yeah! And though this is far from the full story, it is true.

In the 1960s artists came to SoHo and performed "raw space" conversions, meaning that they moved into empty lofts that had been workshops or warehouses and had not been adapted for residential use. Artists got the keys and figured out ways to make do, improvising bathrooms and kitchens and taking advantage of the high ceilings and large windows to stake out studio space. Local restaurant supply stores could provide furnishings and equipment, reinforcing the spaces' existing industrial aesthetic. Some saw SoHo as an opportunity to create new kinds of communities. George Maciunas created Fluxhouse Cooperative, a sort of artist colony. Yoko Ono, among others, came through to perform.

Where the artists went, money followed, and the well-heeled soon pitched their tents downtown and leveled up the local grunge aesthetic. A young architect named Alan Buchsbaum emerged as the designer of choice for the likes of Christie Brinkley, Anna Wintour, Bette Midler, and Diane Keaton; his style was eclectic, collaging influences from pop art, graphic design, and a high-tech style that celebrated the mechanical systems that make modern buildings hum. He splashed in some erotic irreverence, too: "The pre-AIDS seventies—free love, open sex, gay discos, the New York baths scene—was the context for Buchsbaum's own laboratory-for-design lofts," wrote his friend and fellow designer Frederic Schwartz. Color abounded in Buchsbaum's work, as did blown-up photos of blooming roses and industrial lighting paired with giant slabs of marble. Walls were made of glass blocks or, as was the case around actress Ellen Barkin's "bedroom," gauzy curtains. In his own place, he put a hot tub next to where he lay his head.

"I'm not crazy about the cliched New York–style apartment—beige, shiny, and well-coordinated," Buchsbaum reportedly told his friend, art critic Rosalind Krauss, a lion of the downtown scene. "When I design a room, I want people to look at it and ask, 'What's wrong with this picture?'" Canal Street Surrealism is what Krauss dubbed it. The two shared a SoHo building with the sculptor Robert Morris; Buchsbaum designed Krauss's loft, which Janet Malcolm of the *New Yorker* once called "one of the most beautiful living places in New York."

But SoHo didn't stay the province of such rarefied types. In the '70s, loft living went big time. *Life* ran a story extolling the romance of the area to the world. *New York Magazine* proclaimed SoHo the "most exciting place to live in the city," and in its decade-ending issue, writer Marcelle Clements wrote that the loft was "a cultural icon of the seventies" and that its appeal had spread far beyond downtown bohemians.

"It was an extraordinarily exciting time," Joseph Pell Lombardi tells me. "It was an age of discovery."

Lombardi was one of the main architects of loft conversions in New York and designed the conversion of 565 Broadway in 1978. He was "pretty much the go-to guy for SoHo," he says, and Lower

Manhattan is littered with his work. He's also something of a New York City character—the *New York Times* reported that on 9/11 Lombardi took to his penthouse apartment just a block from Ground Zero in a building he had bought and renovated and stayed there while the towers fell. "It was like a captain going to be with his ship," he told the *Times*. He was there for days. "With no phone, he lived off dried fruit and canned tuna, sleeping with a wet mask over his mouth because the apartment was filled with smoke," the *Times* reported.

"The loft that was used for that reality show, in my estimation, is the best loft in New York City or in the world," Lombardi tells me. He acknowledges how strong of a statement that is. "Given the fact that I've probably converted more buildings than anybody else, that has some validity."

Lombardi cites the *Real World* loft's unusually high ceilings, corner location, and well-preserved details, despite it being "probably at its lowest point" when he started working on it. The building had been recently in use, but not by luxury manufacturers and their purveyors. A sewing sweatshop had occupied the second floor, Lombardi says, but the marble floor and cast-iron Corinthian columns remained. It wasn't difficult to clean the space up and turn it back into something luxurious.

It all sounds like a dream—artists and intrepid designers take advantage of a wasteland to reimagine home life, in the process saving forgotten architectural masterpieces and revitalizing a city in decline, and everyone rides off together into a bohemian sunset. Reality was more complicated.

In *Loft Living*, a landmark study that unpacks the complexities of SoHo's transformation and takes away some of the dreamy romance, sociologist Sharon Zukin describes how the transformation of SoHo was part of a larger project led by New York's political and economic elite. "By this late point in capitalist economies probably no real estate market develops without state intervention," she points out.

In other words, plucky young artists didn't transform SoHo alone. Zukin traces the roots of change back to the 1920s, when the Regional Plan Association (RPA), a sort of convocation of influential white people, envisioned clearing Manhattan of industrial spaces. It was an era when urban labor elicited racist fears among Anglo Americans in the country's cities; Black Americans were coming to the urban north as part of the Great Migration, and European immigrants had been arriving with the specter of radical political organizations.

The RPA didn't get its ideas off the ground in the '20s—more than half of the city's manufacturing jobs were in Manhattan even into the '70s, Zukin writes—but starting in 1961, the city used zoning updates to push industry away from Manhattan's residential areas and off the island. A 1975 city code amendment offered tax incentives for residential conversions of large commercial or manufacturing buildings, and many landlords evicted industrial tenants to take advantage of it. Small-scale renovations (cheaper than ground-up construction) in SoHo and the surrounding areas were especially appealing to investors in the '70s, a decade rocked by recession, stagflation, and the near bankruptcy of the city. Artists, even with their kooky ideas about unconventional living, were much less threatening to city fathers than factory workers and their troublesome unions. Plus, the creative wonderland publicized by *Life* and *New York* started attracting tourism—an appealing lifeline for the financially struggling city government.

The conversion of SoHo was also part of a broader transformation of the country. By the '70s, the United States had become a suburban nation, but the white postwar order was falling apart. After Anglos left urban cores en masse and settled in demographically homogeneous suburbs, those families became isolated in little boxes. The suburban escape wasn't turning out to be the promised paradise—I wasn't the only one to find subdivisions full of Caucasians kind of boring, if not soul-crushing. On top of that, President Nixon rolled back federal assistance for low- and middle-income housing, and inflation drove up average single-family home prices, which almost doubled between '74 and '80. Corporations were moving manufacturing jobs overseas, and a new service economy was moving in. The weight of it all was too much. Social support from churches and unions and similar institutions was getting crushed. The crack wasn't just in the picture window; it had spread all the way down to the foundation.

Urban lofts offered a buoyant alternative. They offered a private simulation of a public sphere—"living in a loft is a little like living in a showcase," Zukin wrote ten years before *The Real World* premiered—and among the artists and ghosts of artisans, would-be organization men could cosplay the creative life. SoHo was a playground suffused with the romance and charm of rolling your sleeves up and getting something done, but "only people who do not know the steam and sweat of a real factory can find industrial space romantic," Zukin writes, seemingly with a sneer. "The reason that people develop a sentimental—or a sensual—attachment to the industrial aesthetic is that it is *not* real. To be precise, it is *no longer* real." For an industrial aesthetic to be popular, actual industry and all its messy realities had to be destroyed. "Industry was dead; long live loft living—in its space."

What remained for the white urban colonists was the inconvenience of other people. Thanks to the 1968 Fair Housing Act, which prohibited racial discrimination in the real estate market, even the suburbs weren't safe from racial mixing, and urban cores certainly weren't. Even unofficial segregation was getting harder to pull off. So white people did something clever: They developed a perspective that seemingly embraced the new world order while still confining other races in their service.

Months after *The Real World* premiered, Bill Clinton won the presidency and put together "the most diverse cabinet in history," as the *Washington Post* put it at the time. George H. W. Bush, his predecessor, had appointed only one Black person to his cabinet; Clinton nominated four. After Clinton's inauguration, John Jacob, the president of the National Urban League, said, "There's a feeling that, for the first time in years, the nation has a leader who not only believes in diversity but also is willing to champion it."

Diversity became the buzzword. In the '90s, acclaim for diversity coexisted with racist policies from the politicians who would dominate the next thirty years of American politics: The 1994 Violent Crime Control and Law Enforcement Act, written by then-senator Joe Biden, ushered in the modern age of mass incarceration for Black, Latino, and Native American people; two years later, Clinton signed the Illegal Immigration Reform and Immigrant Responsibility Act, which made it much easier to deport many immigrants; and at the beginning of her three decades in office, California senator Dianne Feinstein wrote a 1993 op-ed in the *Los Angeles Times* that seems to blame immigrants for overcrowding schools and costing taxpayers money. But the 1996 Democratic party platform declared: "We will enter the twenty-first century . . . with the American community coming together, enriched by our diversity and stronger than ever."

Embracing diversity was a way of dealing with the legacy of the Civil Rights Movement after more than a decade of conservative domination of national politics during the Reagan era. For '60s leaders such as Dolores Huerta and Bayard Rustin, racial equity went hand in hand with labor rights. But three successive defeats for Democrats in presidential elections alongside the apparent triumph of capitalist America over the Soviet Union set up Democratic Party strategists to adopt a more business-friendly approach to many things, including racial politics. Exulting diversity was much less threatening than calling for economic justice.

"We needed diversity," Mary-Ellis Bunim and Jon Murray, the creators of *The Real World,* wrote about casting the show in *The Real World: The Ultimate Insider's Guide,* a dishy, behind-the-scenes look at the series. "Drama would come from diversity. Growth would come from diversity. Humor would come from diversity. Heck, diversity would come from diversity."

But diversity wasn't really an end in and of itself. Diversity was good for business.

Pop culture theorist Leigh H. Edwards writes in *The Triumph of Reality TV* that Robert Pittman founded MTV in 1981 to create a "pure environment" to sell ads targeted to young people. The channel embraced a "corporate multiculturalism," Edwards writes, that wouldn't scare off advertisers. Diversity was a paramount concern for *The Real World,* and producers didn't just create diversity in their cast. They gave it architectural form.

"I saw exciting things, weird things," Eric Nies says after being the first person to walk into *The Real World* loft.

The space had the hallmarks of Buchsbaum's interior collages: eclectic furniture in saturated colors, industrial lighting among cast-iron Corinthian columns. There were even some pink curtains around a couple of bare mattresses pushed into a corner—Buchsbaum on a budget.

"I was instructed to come up with an environment that was reactive and creatively expressive—something that encouraged group interaction," the show's production designer, Brian Bigalke, told the *Orlando Sentinel* in '92. The loft's kitchen had mismatched cups and dishes in different colors and materials. It was aestheticized diversity, as though a model of a multiracial society could be made by mixing plastic and glass, and it had more than symbolic value. It created visual interest for the show, interestingness being another of the show's defining features.

"We look for people with interesting histories," says Andrew Hoegl, the casting director for the show's fourth season, in *The Real World: The Ultimate Insider's Guide*. "Those people tend to have interesting things to draw upon and reveal."

At first glance, Hoegl's statement is unremarkable. *Interesting* is a catch-all word, the kind of word you use to describe a book you enjoyed but didn't have any particularly strong feelings about—you learned something but didn't fall in love. But aesthetic theorist Sianne Ngai describes how the seemingly vague word expresses a pervasive experience in modern America. Interesting is an "aesthetic of difference as information," Ngai writes in the book *Our Aesthetic Categories*. The "difference" within interesting things has no particular concept driving it, necessarily, but the mind tries to understand what the difference means, never finding meaning and left to wander across the interesting thing, casually looking for something to hold on to. It's a low-intensity aesthetic, one well suited to '90s liberals looking for moderation.

Diversity, with its inherent differences, is interesting, as life could be in an imagined "diverse" city. An interesting urban experience is a gentle alternative to suburbia. Diversity is not exhilarating or scary or anything else that the social upheaval of the earlier twentieth century might have been. It's less Fritz Lang's *Metropolis*, more Epcot World Showcase. Aestheticized diversity treats race and other social differences as forms of information, abstracted like Buchsbaum's walls in contrasting colors. No hue is better or worse or more important. No shade is freighted with a historical meaning. The colors are just different, and isn't it nice to see them together? Isn't it interesting?

This framework, of course, most benefits white people.

Experiences on *The Real World* tend to edify white roommates, usually at the expense of Black ones. The first season centers on Julie Gentry, a young white woman leaving Alabama to explore the world, and her habits and expectations contrast with those of the people around her. She asks her roommate Heather B. Gardner, a Black woman, if she sells drugs because she has a beeper and tells another Black roommate, Kevin Powell, that he's "very bitter" after he says that "racism is alive and well." But she learns and grows, eventually accepting her new friends.

The narrative arc of the conservative white person discovering the world repeats over the seasons. "The beauty about this experience is the fact of being challenged by people that are very different from myself," says Aaron Behle, a white man on season 2. Trishelle Cannatella, a white woman on *The Real World: Las Vegas*, is excited to live with people of different races, "excited to learn."

Powell's arc, however, also recurs. He was socially isolated on the show, and on many seasons, the roommates talk about kicking out a Black male roommate, either because he's "aggressive" or supposedly doesn't work hard enough or makes them feel "uncomfortable."

The Real World has a running thread of white terror. On the Washington, D. C., season, a white woman demands that a Black male roommate leave the house if he doesn't stop drinking at home, and when he talks about feeling ganged up on and isolated, she cries and says that she's not "trying to be the bad guy." On the Austin, Texas, season, Rachel Moyal says she hopes Nehemiah Clark "gets shot on the street one day" after they fight. In the second New Orleans season, a white roommate, Ryan Leslie, calls the cops on Preston Roberson-Charles after a routine spat in the house. "I think Preston's really scared, and I think that's awesome," Leslie says about the cops' arrival.

Aestheticized diversity on-screen minimizes the intensity of lived diversity, making it something a passive audience can easily manage. White audiences can sit back and distance themselves from the visceral intensity of racism performed by bad actors. *They are the problem. They are bothered by Black people. I find Black people to be a delight. I would never call the cops on Black men. Black people are different, sure, but that difference isn't scary; it's interesting.* With this perspective, a Southerner like Gentry becomes a vehicle for others to offload racism onto. It's similar to how *Selling Sunset* sets up its realtors as dodos to look down on in order to reassure viewers of their own superiority.

The Real World's vision of diversity was a reprieve from other unsettling videos of Black men flooding airwaves at the time. The show premiered just weeks after the trial of the police officers who beat Rodney King, an unarmed Black man, in Los Angeles. A bystander caught the violence in a recording that was replayed in news segments around the world, and the acquittal of the officers ignited an uprising that gripped the country. These seven strangers in SoHo presented TV audiences with a very different fantasy of racial coexistence and a much more soothing presence to invite into white living rooms.

The show didn't just offer pleasant distraction. Like *Selling Sunset,* it changed audiences' relationship with the wider world. On *The Real World,* racism is a matter of ignorance cured by exposure to different people. Exposure to diversity, the show seems to say, can change people. It can create something new. Diversity lofts have generative potential. In them, life can be productive even if there's nothing traditionally productive happening. Just hanging out with friends can be productive if it's caught on tape, a chance to forge a marketable identity. The show laid out a template for anyone to record their home and turn it digital and make a lot of money in the process.

By the time I started watching *The Real World* in the late '90s, it had started to drift from its starting point. In the beginning, the show cast talented young people trying to make it in their careers, whether they were writers, med students, or political cartoonists. We'd see them go to auditions, interview for jobs, and volunteer with local communities. But by my day, it was much more about watching bodies in action—fighting, fucking, or both. In-house hot tubs became standard, along with cutouts in the shower walls, and roommates toasted their arrivals to the house by saying things like, "Here's to making new friends and having a huge seven-person orgy."

Was I enjoying the diversity? Yes, but I was also enjoying the titillation provided by my new hot and horny friends.

Rewatching the first seasons is almost painful—young singers, rappers, and artists walk onto MTV and get a golden opportunity to break through, but they're almost all bad at self-promotion or just refuse to do it. On the first season, Andre Comeau seems almost embarrassed for his band to be on the show—embarrassed for his garage band to get a national audience on MTV—as though he were selling out or posing.

Now, it seems that hardly anyone goes on a reality show without a packaged personal brand ready for rollout, and the late *Real World* seasons have an influencer-factory vibe. Roommates who do the most fighting and fucking go on to become low-level social media stars or get roles on one of the *Challenge* competition show spin-offs or even graduate to other networks. (Karamo Brown was on the Philadelphia season and eventually became a host on Bravo's *Queer Eye*; CT Tamburello was on the Paris season and won the second season of *The Traitors* with Cannatella.) Though producers started giving the casts group jobs on season five, those workplaces were really just sets where the cast was forced to interact. The real work was performing an identity that could win over an audience. Going on the show and living in front of cameras became a job in itself.

Zukin writes about an early cliche of loft living being "urban homesteading"—pioneers camping out in cleared-out spaces—but she argues it was more like subsistence housing. Artists supported themselves using what they created in their homes. Unlike the factory workers who created silverware and mantelpieces and whatever else in these spaces and then went home, artists made art there and stuck around to sleep and eat and do whatever else. The Real Worlders continued that tradition and took it a step further. They made "art," or entertainment, in their loft *while* sleeping and eating and doing whatever else. They erased any boundaries between their work and their personal lives; the two became one. And ultimately, The Real Worlders' focus shifted from making the show to making themselves. Their identities became the products, and products had to be associated with good brands.

On the second-to-last season, Mike Crescenzo, a white man, freaks out after making a racist joke on camera while drunk and decides to go home the same night. When a roommate asks him what's wrong, he tells them, "It has to do with, I think, like, how I'm gonna be, like, portrayed." During a cast discussion about race on the last season, which ran in 2019, a Black roommate asks white roommates why they don't voice opinions on "Black issues," and one white roommate responds: "Do you know how much [bleeped] we would get as white women in America? Any opinion we have will be [bleeped] on . . . I didn't want to be disrespectful ever."

Diversity is good for personal business as well as corporate business, and it's good for the business of cities, too. Since the '90s, technocrats have seized on diversity and its accompanying creativity as solutions for struggling metropolises. In 2002 economist Richard Florida published *The Rise of the Creative Class*, which argued that diversity drove creativity and was a key ingredient of the contemporary economic success of cities like San Francisco and Boston. The idea became a touchstone for technocratic ways of thinking invested in urban living.

Even people averse to that kind of capitalist boosterism have valorized diversity and creativity. In *The Gentrification of the Mind*, a memoir of life in New York during the height of the AIDS epidemic, writer and activist Sarah Schulman decries the bourgeois, homogeneous masses with a "hypnotic identification with authority" who moved into lower Manhattan while its gay population was dying. The newcomers lack the "diversity of thought and experiences that produces a dynamic mutual exposure to varied points of view," she writes. "Gentrification is the removal of the dynamic mix that defines urbanity—the familiar interaction of different kinds of people creating ideas together . . . the daily affirmation that people from other experiences are real makes innovative solutions and experiments possible."

Diversity is productive, generative. It innervates. The energy of different people colliding supplies the spark of life.

But this rosy idea of urban diversity is just as much of a romantic fantasy as the idea that artists magically resuscitated SoHo on their own. What diversity actually generates is a stable economy under white control, untroubled by radical politics.

A celebration of diversity does not translate to a redistribution of power. White people across New York are now moving into historically Black neighborhoods such as Harlem and Bedford-Stuyvesant, driving up home prices in some of the last relatively affordable pockets of the city and displacing local communities while making the areas more "diverse." And much of modern SoHo is built on what some consider to be the first community of free Black people in North America, created by people formerly enslaved in New Amsterdam. The English effectively destroyed the community in the seventeenth and eighteenth centuries, enabling it to become a white commercial wonderland in the nineteenth.

Now, urban planners and developers see diversity as an asset to be exploited. A pattern emerges, Zukin writes: "power *in* diversity and power *over* diversity."

Julie Gentry walked into the first *Real World* loft and created a new, marketable identity by learning from the diverse group around her. The country followed.

—

Alan Buchsbaum died of AIDS complications in 1987. Bette Midler sang at his memorial. Rosalind Krauss has since remodeled her home. Robert Morris moved out of his; now "it's owned by Jack Dorsey, if you can believe it," Krauss tells me. But the appeal of loft living endures. After the aesthetic spread across Manhattan in the '70s, it kept going across the country. In the inaugural issue of *Dwell* in 2000, design critic Mimi Zeiger wrote about "the lofting of America."

Zeiger finds lofts marketed in cities large and small across the country. She quotes a West Coast developer, who appreciates the "individualism" of lofts, and a real estate marketer who says that lofts appeal to "young, single professionals who have recently moved to Atlanta from California and New York and are working toward middle management at Merrill Lynch . . . yet they want to retain the urban atmosphere that they are used to." Who says you can't have it all? Now, young corporate professionals can choose between the Lofts on 16th Condos in Anchorage, Ola Ka 'Ilima Artspace Lofts in Honolulu, and the Parc Lofts in Miami.

After the first season, *The Real World* shot in many postindustrial spaces: a pier in Seattle, a warehouse in Austin, another warehouse in Atlanta. "SoHo in New York begat SoMa, south of Market Street, in San Francisco, SoWa, south of Washington Street, in Boston, SoDo, south of Downtown, in Seattle and SoFo, south of Folkungagatan, in Stockholm," Zukin writes. "SoHos are now made, not born." The same could be said of the new SoHos' denizens, striving so hard to produce marketable identities.

"Know who you are and deliver it at all times," RuPaul Charles advises not only contestants on *RuPaul's Drag Race* but anyone else listening. It's a sort of extension of "know thyself," the ancient advice of the Delphic oracle, for the personal branding age. The work of delivering yourself is never done. On-screen identities may be the most valuable work products of many people's lives, critical to finding a job, meeting a mate, staying in touch with family, or getting any kind of social approval.

Since 2020, especially, corporate and political discussions supporting diversity have extended to include equity and inclusion in attempts to at least nod to more substantive change that doesn't just appeal to white gazes, but the pushback under Trump's administration has been punishing. "Diversity" has become a favorite conservative straw man, but it's such an easy target because it was a flimsy concept to begin with. And even though diversity is now not so explicitly chic in left-leaning circles, the concept and its supposed benefits still shape how many people think about cities and homes.

These days, diversity lofts abound on TV. The generation of shows that appeared around 2000, including *Survivor* and *Big Brother*, took the formula further, adding structured competition to the premise but still essentially creating entertainment by forcing diverse groups to interact in a limited space. On the forty-sixth season of *Survivor*, which aired in 2024, contestant Charlie Davis, a young white man, tells the camera, "On *Survivor*, you've got people from every single walk of life, every single background, and I'm just really excited to learn people's stories and, you know, pop that bubble."

Diversity lofts create sanitized SoHos of the mind. Like homes in the Hollywood Hills, they provide feelings of power and security for white people. The interesting charms of diversity linger in them along with the rest of the fantasies of the neoliberal '90s in a world that's obsessed with work. Hybrid homes give these latent impulses room to spread and silently shape our lives.

The Real World may have ended in 2019, but the universe the show created evolves and endures. *The Real World* is dead; long live reality.

Get your fucking ass up and work

Part of diversity's appeal for white people has been that people of color, Black and Native American people especially, are supposedly more "real," more "authentic," and people seem to think that hanging out with them will make life more whole. Since long before the days of Norman Mailer rhapsodizing about the residents of Harlem, white people have found the electrifying feeling of "the real world" in jazz, traditional ceremonies, and anything that smacks of a "simpler" way of life, one supposedly more embodied or guided by emotion and intuition and enriched by hard, immediate sensory experiences. Overlapping with this are other fantasies. Some romanticize "real" work, physical labor whereby people enjoy what they make with their own two hands—work that is increasingly done by non-white people. There are also notions about real love, best practiced by people who live close to the earth and not in the alienating cities and towers where white-collar workers punch clocks.

All these dreams are built into America's physical homes, which fossilize immaterial impulses into something permanent and tangible. Architecture is more than frozen music—it's frozen biases and attitudes, feelings and fears given form. Now, hybrid homes are changing things up a bit. The abstract cultural threads frozen in architecture sublimate with a little digital heat, and their forces and trajectories become harder to trace in a liquid world.

Reality TV homes may come at a critical juncture between the old physical world that we can pin down and wrestle with and the new world that swirls around us, out of our fingers, suffocating us with ease. Changing the direction of our hybrid homes may be our only chance for survival before our digital technology and the people directing it overwhelm us.

In this confusing new landscape, even seemingly benign experiences can be freighted with malice.

The 1950s picture windows that used to connect living rooms to the wider world have long since turned into televisions and other screens, and the people on those devices offer a form of companionship in increasingly isolated homes. But in hybrid homes this companionship blends with the spirit of competition underlying the design of physical homes. Even what seems like just hanging out with a surrogate family actually trains your brain to compete with everyone and hide from threats as if you're hunkered down in a bunker or, as the case may be for one famous family, your farmhouse.

Competition has been part of reality TV since the start of its modern age with the summer of *Survivor* in 2000, when the surprise hit dominated ratings and the zeitgeist while pioneering forms of product placement and ad sales that changed the industry. Shows such as *Big Brother* raised the stakes of *The Real World* fishbowl format by forcing the people on the show to vote each other off one by one, and a wave of more competition-oriented hits, such as *American Idol* and *The Bachelor*, defined early 2000s reality TV by focusing less on the fishbowl and more on the striving. Even noncompetitive home renovation or makeover shows in the Y2K reality TV golden age had an air of competition: time pressure, divided teams, limited resources, and conclusions that were either rapturous or disappointing. This feeling survived even after the competition show craze died down.

A hit show on MTV that premiered in 2002 would augur the next phase of reality TV, which was ostensibly a return to *The Real World* documentary model—watch some people in a house interact and live their unstructured lives. But this show was different. It reworked the potentially sleepy format of following people around with cameras and waiting for something to happen by focusing for many seasons on a specific and unusual group of people: aging rocker Ozzy Osbourne, his wife, Sharon, and two of their kids, Jack and Kelly.

The first episode starts with a voiceover. "Meet the perfect American family," it says, and introduces the gang in between clips of Kelly calling Jack a "fucking loser" and Sharon telling the kids to "shut the fuck up and go to bed" and Ozzy thrusting his hips against a dog's backside.

"There Goes the Neighborhood," the episode is titled, and it shows the family moving into a Beverly Hills mansion. "This has got to be the twenty-fourth house that my kids have lived in," Sharon says. The family unpacks crucifixes, has painters stencil crosses on the walls, and hangs a horned devil on the front door, while supposed neighbors watch with crossed arms. Ozzy complains that thanks to new technology he needs a computer to turn on his TV. "Fucking space-age shit," he mumbles before telling his son that the multifunctional remote should also provide blow jobs. The two end up settling in to watch a History Channel show about World War II.

The Real World and *An American Family* dramatized differences of opinion and colliding cultural and personal beliefs and developed storylines about divorce, conservatives disagreeing with liberals, etcetera. They were less like the 1950s patriarchal family sitcoms and more like the '70s shows created by Norman Lear that pit out-of-touch, conservative fathers against savvy, liberal kids. *The Osbournes* winked at that idea—its theme song was a jazzy, Frank Sinatra–style rendition of Ozzy's hit "Crazy Train," with lyrics wondering if millions of people can learn to love each other—and the show incorporated some family sitcom structure, with bickering children, a bumbling father, and nagging mother, but it didn't have a sitcom's linear approach to storytelling.

"Most reality shows have a narrative arc, and they always had the principals talking to camera and saying, I was feeling really mad when Sabrina did X or Y," Brian Graden, who was president at MTV when the show started, tells me. "And we tried that, and it was the most boring show because there was nothing linear about the logic of the Osbournes."

The Osbournes ended up being more like a collection of short videos than a traditional show.

"It wasn't the story that was interesting," Graden says. "It was the fact that they threw ham at their neighbors over the fence, period. Or it was the fact that Ozzy was vacuuming, period. And so we decided to abandon every convention, took out all the sound bites, took out any attempted story, and just made it little vignettes. So a lot of times, act two after the commercial had absolutely nothing to do with act one. We just cut to him now on laughing gas. But that was the right realization for that show."

The result was chaotic. *The Osbournes* reveled in the breakdown of traditional order in both its storytelling structure and its content. It was a kind of devolution of the *Brady Bunch* trajectory: the once-cheery children now grown and rebellious, the father bumbling, addled by years of hard living, comically unprepared for the wild new millennium he's forced to deal with and domineered by a sharper, more savvy wife. Ozzy was hardly a father who knows best; he often seemed to barely know enough to make it through his day.

"Everybody had a celeb-reality show after that," Graden says, and he's basically right, if "everybody" refers to a certain section of the rich and fame-ish. *The Anna Nicole Show* premiered later in 2002; *Newlyweds: Nick & Jessica* in 2003; *Run's House, Being Bobby Brown,* and *Britney and Kevin: Chaotic* in 2005; *Kimora: Life in the Fab Lane* two years later.

And all this might never have happened if it weren't for a piece of architecture: the Osbournes' old family home. In 2000, MTV began airing *Cribs,* a show that took cameras inside the homes of celebrities. Its first episode featured the Osbournes, and, as Graden tells it, the magic of Ozzy teasing Kelly about an NSYNC poster on her wall inspired producers to take a shot.

Nina L. Diaz, who created *Cribs,* told the *New York Post* that the Osbournes had "the most classic house" on the show, a different mansion. "They had the oil paintings, full settings in the dining room, red velvet furniture, Baroque mixed with different things," Diaz said. "They had the most adult house."

Not all of the houses on the show followed such familiar domestic organizations. On one of the show's most famous episodes, Mariah Carey shows off a lingerie closet, a room for her bathtub with a sitting area and TV, and a fainting couch in the kitchen before donning four-inch heels and climbing a stair machine in her private gym. In the second season, Jermaine Dupri takes audiences through his 5,000-square-foot suburban Atlanta home, which he says is "getting ready to be the craziest bachelor pad you have ever been to in your life." The show intercuts shots of his home with music video clips of women in bikinis and ends the tour at his garage, where he shows his cars: two Ferraris, a Bentley, a Mercedes, and a Range Rover.

"Jermaine Dupri embraced it because that's the aesthetic of hip-hop: the braggadocio, the status," Diaz told the *Washington Post.* "The hip-hop community gave us so much love in the beginning," she told the *New York Post.* "They were very proud of what they had."

Cribs, and particularly the hip-hop stars on it, subverted any lingering baby boomer notions of the suburbs as a place for demure conformity. In that way, the show exemplified what writer Ariel Levy called raunch culture and the accompanying indie sleaze aesthetic, which often juxtaposed overt sexuality with suburban backgrounds. Although raunch and indie sleaze were usually very white and 2000s hip-hop was predominantly Black, both worlds embraced irony by touting markers of success, such as expensive cars, clothing, and houses, while eschewing baby boomer standards of propriety and modesty, often in misogynistic ways. The movements seemingly thumbed their noses at the rhetoric coming from the Republican-led federal government, led by George W. Bush, an evangelical Christian seemingly obsessed with patriotism and "traditional values."

Producers of *The Osbournes* consciously reacted to that conservative context.

"Sitcoms had always been family-based or mostly family- or work-based up until then," Graden says. "And so we were trying to evoke a sense of family. And if you remember, that was kind of the George Bush era where he was trying to define family values in a certain very right-wing way. And so we kind of wanted to say, every family is different and you can't tell me this family loves each other any less than any other kind."

But around 2007, the Y2K era of reality started to wind down when this conservative suburban context started to change and was no longer an effective foil.

The end began in the home: A bubble in the domestic housing market burst, and the ensuing subprime mortgage crisis triggered millions of foreclosures across the country. The global economy slid into recession. Suburbia was no longer a frothy playground, the default backdrop for sleazy teenage dreams, but a landscape of ruin and despair. The end of the rollicking golden age of reality TV was the end of the golden age of the American Dream of single-family homeownership.

At the same time, the entertainment industry was roiled by economic changes of its own. Networks ordered more unscripted shows to cut costs, and the 2007 Writers Guild of America strike reminded executives of the relative security of relying on largely nonunion reality shows.

In this evolving entertainment ecosystem, reality TV was a young species with a lot of potential to develop and fill new niches left vacant by dying scripted dinosaurs. The genre could provide much more than competition shows, as the celeb-reality shows had been demonstrating.

An early volunteer in the new landscape was *Jersey Shore*, another MTV hit, which premiered in 2009 and followed a group of twentysomethings, most Italian American, spending a summer in a house together in the New Jersey beach party town of Seaside Heights. It was the brainchild of executive Shelly Tatro.

"The original format she had was *America's Next Top Guido*," Graden tells me. "This was her title, not mine." But plans for the show shifted away from competition, and one of the most popular documentary style shows of the 2010s was born.

The competition format was so tired that one of the most successful competition shows to launch in this era was a parody. *Drag Race*, which started in 2009, lampooned the idea of performers competing for stardom or, in this case, to be "America's next drag superstar." At the time, it was laughable that such a thing could possibly exist.

The Real World developed the idea that anyone could work in show business just by going about their lives on camera, and competition shows pushed the idea that anyone could become a working "star." *The Osbournes* and other celebrity series inverted that progression, turning stars into regular people who would bicker, joke, eat, and do myriad other Joe Schmo things on camera. The sense of competition became less overt, but it was still in reality TV's DNA, transmuted into a constant fight for attention, where performers clamored with every inane skit or stunt for camera time.

And during this time of change, when old dreams of a peaceful suburban paradise dimmed, a new star rose, calling the country to embrace hope. Barack Obama brought a triumphalist feeling of change to the 2008 election, resurrecting dreams of equality from the 1960s just as the previous decade resurrected dreams of domesticity from the '50s.

The ensuing Obama era inverted cultural standards of the Bush years and what came before. Striving for conventional success became cool again. Hipster irony was out, and earnestness and authenticity were in. Working hard to get ahead no longer had to be cloaked beneath layers of affected slouching, but the new work was different. It wasn't laboring for a company all your life and climbing up the ladder. It was a time to be clever and work smarter, not harder. Facebook and other tech start-ups brought the rise of the wunderkinds, twentysomethings who skyrocketed to record-breaking fortunes while debt-laden boomers skidded to the curb. Explanations of the mortgage crisis and subsequent recession are often inscrutable to anyone not fluent in the financial jargon of collateralized debt obligations, mortgage-backed securities, credit default swaps, and derivatives. Maverick economic wizards now wore the crown in the increasingly liquid world; the dutiful union knights lost the castle. The prevailing wisdom was: Drop out of college and launch a start-up. Being a cog in the machine won't get you anywhere because the machine is broken. Disrupt it.

Make money, do good, and change the world—the millennial sensibility didn't turn away from competition but embraced those who competed more savvily than their forebears. A few canny upstarts recognized that fame and fortune were available to anyone who could treat their identities like start-ups.

Before Diaz created *Cribs*, there was *Lifestyles of the Rich and Famous*, created by Alfred Masini. In 1981 Masini also started *Entertainment Tonight*, the tabloid show that focuses on celebrity news, a topic that would find a new home at the cable channel E!. There, executives seemed hungry for anything that would offer audiences a closer look at the rich and famous or could-be-famous. On E!, a new show would pick up the legacy of *The Osbournes* and eventually usher in the era of the girlboss, when even a raunchy young woman could grow and take control of the economic system and media ecosystem that had exploited her body using a savvy that her elders would not even recognize as a form of economic intelligence.

"Not bad for a girl with no talent."

What does life look like when even hanging out with friends can become not just work but a competition? It's not a loft or a slick glass mansion that's showing the way forward, but a farmhouse, of all things—albeit a modern one.

Soaring over the Pacific, then the hills of Southern California before descending over a backyard pool, a drone flies through musician Travis Barker's legs and into a mansion in Calabasas. It's the opening of season 1 of *The Kardashians*, the Hulu version of the famous family's flagship reality TV show. With slick editing, an airborne camera weaves in and out of Kourtney's, Khloé's, Kendall's, Kris's, Kylie's, and Kim's homes and offices, showing the stars going about their days before a barbecue at Kim's house. It's a thrilling sequence, not only because of the camera's aerial gymnastics but because it promises that the new series will continue developing the seamless intimacy of their earlier show on E!, *Keeping Up with the Kardashians*. Since that show premiered in 2007, the Kardashian-Jenners have sold a form of companionship by welcoming audiences into their homes, and millions have shared in the family's journey from their chaotic first-season house with a porch and a stripper pole to Kim and Kanye's minimalist mausoleum and beyond. In the Hulu series, Kris and Khloé have taken the show's vision of togetherness further, moving into neighboring homes so that family will always be just a few steps away.

But as I watched this development in 2022, something tripped me up: Kris and Khloé were moving into modern farmhouses. The style, though trendy at the time, seemed a puzzling choice. I associate modern farmhouses with HGTV, Chip and Joanna Gaines, shiplap and old books, decorative metal pitchers that look like Clara Barton might've used them to dress a gangrenous wound—nostalgia, not navigating what's new, as the Kardashian-Jenners have historically done so well. Granted, the interiors of Kris's and Khloé's homes aren't very rustic; Khloé's is minimalist, monochrome, and beige, its wide plank floors the only thing vaguely reminiscent of farm life. Kris's a bit more traditional with a few pieces of reclaimed wooden furniture, but the interior, shaped by celebrity designers Kathleen Clements, Tommy Clements, and Waldo Fernandez, is so large and sparsely decorated that it looks more like the presidential suite at a high-end resort than a folksy family retreat. There's not an apron sink in sight in either. But on the outside of both, the farmhouse style is unmistakable: piles of simple, low-slung forms covered in batten board and stone tile, a mix of materials that I suppose is meant to look old and like it was accumulated over decades. Looking at them, I wondered if the queens of the future might be winding down their reign and preparing to retreat, at least stylistically, into the past.

But that narrative might be too simple. Talking to Laura Barraclough, chair of the American Studies department at Yale and author of *Making the San Fernando Valley*, I learn that the idea of living in a modern farmhouse is nothing new—it has deep roots in the Valley, where the Kardashians live. "It fits with the history of that place," she tells me. "There's a wider aesthetic that supports what they are doing." Time and again people in the United States and especially in Southern California have conjured a fantasy of homesteading to escape the dehumanizing effects of modern life, though the promise of personal freedom and prosperity often comes at some dramatic societal expense.

A century ago, the writer Ralph Borsodi promoted the back-to-the-land movement to urban professionals disenchanted with the grind of life in big cities, exacerbated by the 1920–1921 depression. He opens his 1933 book, *Flight from the City*, with a narrative that feels familiar today. He and his family were living in New York City, where a housing shortage made rents "outrageously high," and his family was too caught up in trying to survive to savor the fruits of the metropolis.

"How could we enjoy them when we were financially insecure and never knew when we might be without a job?" he wrote. Then, in 1920, the house they rented was sold and they had no place to live. Instead of sticking it out in the big city, they gave up and moved to a small plot on the outskirts, where they set up a homestead with a small farmhouse and land where they could grow and raise their own food. It was a lot of work, but Borsodi discovered that homesteading could create a more economically secure and "expressive" way of life.

Borsodi was optimistic about farmhouse living as a way to free people from their dependence on massive markets. He wasn't wild about either capitalism or socialism. Both, he thought, made people dependent on forces far beyond them. "Insecurity is the price we pay for our dependence upon industrialism for the essentials of life," he wrote. Homesteading, for him, wasn't just a nostalgic idealization of the past; it was a way to manifest a better destiny built on self-reliance, independence, and other ideals grounded in frontier living.

The historical connection to the Kardashian-Jenners gets clearer when I talk to Tomer Fridman, Kris and Khloé's real estate agent. He echoes Barraclough and tells me that modern farmhouses make a lot of sense in the strange city where the two live: Hidden Hills. Incorporated in 1961, it is a guard-gated city—one of the few in the United States, Fridman says—and it's an equestrian community, meaning that it has zoning laws requiring space for stables on individual properties and public bridle paths maintained by the city. "If you go there, you feel like you're on a ranch," Fridman tells me. "You see kids riding their horses to school or parents taking their kids on horseback. Granted, it could be, like, LeAnn Rimes, but it's still horseback."

Fridman impresses upon me that Hidden Hills is not Calabasas, which is something that has always confused me, as the Kardashian-Jenners seem to refer to them interchangeably on the show. The twin cities sit across from each other on opposite sides of the 101 freeway at the western end of the San Fernando Valley. Kim, Khloé, Kris, Kylie, and Rob are in Hidden Hills; Kourtney is the only one in Calabasas. "Hidden Hills was always what I would call old money," Fridman says. Calabasas is newer, incorporated in 1991, and larger, with about 22,000 people compared with Hidden Hills's 1,700. Calabasas is not a gated city, just one full of gated communities. "In Calabasas, you don't have the contemporary farmhouse. Hidden Hills is a traditional community. It looks more like the Palisades or the Hamptons. Calabasas looks like Beverly Park. It has a grander feel . . . Calabasas looks like Newport Coast, like Orange County."

Crucially, however, they are both independent from the city of Los Angeles. Like other wealthy enclaves in the LA area, such as Beverly Hills, they offer rich people a way to be close to the city without sharing its financial burdens. And life behind the gates offers the promise of security, or at least privacy from tourists and paparazzi.

According to Fridman, the first modern farmhouse in Hidden Hills appeared around 2013. It was a renovation of an old Cape Cod–style home recently vacated by a family looking for more room—coincidentally, the Kardashian-Jenners. This was the house Kris and Caitlyn lived in on their first three seasons on TV, and after they sold it, the new owners renovated it into the first of a new style, at least in the area. "I'd never seen anything like it," Fridman says. "Not in the city, not in the Valley, not in the Hills, not anywhere. It was done by an architect named George De La Nuez, and he's ended up completely transforming Hidden Hills since that house."

Ranch and Cape Cod style homes had traditionally dominated the city, but the new style was sweeping in. "I would see my house copied everywhere," De La Nuez tells me. (De La Nuez did not design Kris's and Khloé's new homes; Kris's was designed by Brian Lerman, according to De La Nuez, and Khloé's by Ryan Levis, both architects with offices in Southern California.) "I think a part of it is that it's almost the first style that hit during the Instagram and social media phase. Everything gets spread to everybody so quickly." But De La Nuez says, "The best examples are certainly in Hidden Hills," where height limitations intended to maintain a rural feel along with prohibitions against flat roofs mean that developers trying to maximize the allowable built square footage on lots have to break up homes into rambling accumulations of smaller volumes. (Were any portion of a home's footprint ever to reach the grand dimensions of, say, a pseudo French château, there would be no way a pitched roof could cover it and stay below the thirty-foot ridge height limit.) "I think it's popular also because it's easy to build," De La Nuez says. "There's not much articulation to it. It's simple, it's materials like batten board siding or James Hardie plank siding, so you have the wood siding. You have stone accents that basically anybody can execute."

There's a relative humility to the style, too, though I emphasize the word *relative*, as the modern farmhouses in Hidden Hills regularly sell for upward of $5 million. "There's not a lot of grand approaches," De La Nuez says. "You don't have the monumental gates and the pilasters and the big-ass light fixtures . . . It's not a screaming, look-at-me kind of house . . . They still have their Bentleys in the driveway, but Hidden Hills is a community that does not celebrate pompousness. There's people on horseback riding around, looking into your backyard . . . You're out on your front porch. You can say hi to neighbors walking by."

This fantasy of rural-suburban living goes back locally even further than the incorporation of Hidden Hills in the 1960s to the '20s, the same time when Borsodi was promoting the back-to-the-land movement outside New York. Los Angeles leaders were eager to market their city as an alternative to the polluted, congested cities of the Midwest and East Coast, which were attracting many emigrants from southern and eastern Europe and turning into hotbeds of working-class discontent. LA leaders touted their city as the "white spot," the reward for

Anglos for crossing and conquering the continent, and they set out plans for a decentralized city where the working population would be dispersed and less likely to congregate and organize for labor rights.

Developers also targeted affluent whites with dreams of starting over on impractically small farms that would offer an escape from urban hustle, bustle, and ethnic mixing. Journalist William Smythe organized what he called Little Landers colonies across Southern California, some in the Valley, and recruited white urbanites to move onto small lots, raise chickens, and grow crops. It was an attractive fantasy, never mind that Japanese American, Chinese American, and Mexican American laborers were often the ones making the area's many farms succeed and were barred from buying into these projects.

Barraclough tells me that interest in homesteading in the San Fernando Valley generally and the Calabasas area specifically resurged in the 1960s, '70s, and '80s. Community groups organized events where white-collar professionals effectively donned *Little House on the Prairie* drag. This was also when tract homes were sprawling across the Valley, destroying the remains of the older, larger-lot homes, and when fair housing laws were passed, meaning people of color could legally move into more parts of the city. Many white people got nostalgic for a time they'd never experienced and that probably wasn't a whole lot like what they imagined.

Early ads for Hidden Hills homes promised "Your Own Rancho" and featured prop wagons. Fridman remembers that in the early '90s there was a stagecoach on display in Old Town Calabasas. "It was like the Wild West," he says.

So maybe Kris and Khloé just happen to live in a style of home that's very popular in their area—an idea I have trouble accepting, given that the Kardashian-Jenners are no strangers to renovations—but why do they live in Hidden Hills, anyway?

—

When Kris first visited Hidden Hills, she "saw horses, llamas, and cows, and people walking their dogs and riding their horses," she writes in her 2011 memoir, *Kris Jenner . . . and All Things Kardashian*. "It was heaven."

As she writes it, Kris went to Hidden Hills to start over. It was 1996. She had divorced her first husband, celebrity lawyer Robert Kardashian, and had married the former Olympian whom we now know as Caitlyn Jenner. Kris's life with Caitlyn was markedly different: Robert was wealthy, and Caitlyn, an athlete whose endorsement deals and acting gigs were drying up, was less so. Kris and Caitlyn were struggling to support their large family, and Kris was beginning the career pivot that would change the nature of celebrity as we know it. But first, they needed a place to live.

Hidden Hills gave Kris a launchpad. Throughout the '90s, Kris revived Caitlyn's job prospects, steering the former athlete toward speaking gigs, infomercials, and more. It was in this pseudo-rural city that Kris honed the craft of parlaying someone's name recognition into a monetizable career, and her urgency to work only increased in 2003, when her ex-husband, father of four of her children, died.

"It's a profound moment when your children lose a parent and you are the only parent left. It was up to me then to help them make something of their lives," Kris writes. "I had realized my lifelong dream of having six kids, and now I was done with the birthing and ready for the work. It was time to stop screwing around. It was time to get off my ass and get to work."

A few years later, after her second-eldest daughter, Kim, achieved minor celebrity status thanks to her friendship with Paris Hilton and eventual notoriety, Kris made the most of the moment and pitched a reality show about her family in the style of *The Osbournes*—the shrewd mother married to an aloof spouse, both struggling to keep up with their unruly kids—to Ryan Seacrest and producers at E! The producers said yes, *Keeping Up with the Kardashians* began, and Kris's life as a "momager" took off.

Suddenly, the activity within Kris's home, recorded and distributed to a global audience, became the source of the family's income. As in an artist loft or on a homestead, home life was "work" life. Hidden Hills aligned with that fantasy in a way that areas such as Beverly Hills or the Hollywood Hills, domestic retreats from urban office culture, would not have. Kris was on her way to helping advance a new type of domestic life for the new millennium's hybrid homes with an accompanying architecture. Early Real Worlders fumbled through proto-influencer lifestyles, and *Selling Sunset* realtors have nominally held on to their job of selling homes, but Kris's clan really pioneered what it means to work in a digital farmhouse.

The early seasons of *KUWTK* play up the idea of the overworked housewife/manager/mother with storylines involving a lot of improbable, presumably staged scenarios that leave the stars struggling to accomplish some task: Kris feels like an empty nester, so her kids get her a monkey as a surrogate child, and she has to take care of it; Kris accidentally distributes a racy calendar Kim made for her boyfriend, and Kim has to run around town to get all the calendars out of stores. The show has an *I Love Lucy* vibe with Kris as Lucy, constantly trying to break into showbiz by trying and failing to do odd jobs while also performing the unpaid work of being a housewife and mother. As the seasons progress, the zany antics ebb and bigger dramas—divorces, births, extramarital affairs—swell, but the side plots endure and get even less purposeful. In season 14, Kris hires a scribe to follow her around and record every word she says. Later that season, the kids handcuff Kris to a mime, Pierre, and she has to go about her day with him in tow.

"Zaniness is as much about desperate laboring as playful fun," Sianne Ngai writes in *Our Aesthetic Categories*. Zaniness is an aesthetic of what Ngai calls "on-demand post-Fordism," where people are juggling gigs and side hustles, families and Zoom calls, professional Instagrams and personal brand–building. Though zany comedy is funny for the audience, it's not much fun for the zany character, who is overworking to the point of failure.

Modern farmhouses aren't particularly zany, and screwball comedy is definitely not what gentleman farmers had in mind when they imagined living off the land, but in the first few seasons of the show, the Kardashian-Jenners weren't living in a modern farmhouse. They were living in an "adorable Cape Cod all-American dream," as Kris puts it in her memoir. The Cape Cod style, De La Nuez says, was popular in Hidden Hills at the time, and it has its own associations with work ethic—it was the style of Levittown, redolent of economy, modesty, and hardscrabble Puritans focused on God and self-reliance and freedom from the state—and the first house lent itself to the show's original vibe. The Cape Cod style's postwar suburban associations aligned with Kris's vision of the family as a "modern-day Brady Bunch," a blend of Kris's kids with Robert Kardashian and those with Caitlyn Jenner. Compared with the mammoth dimensions of their later homes, the spaces in this initial home are small, cluttered with furniture, kitschy bric-a-brac, and people. Camera shots feel chaotic and haphazardly composed; some weird painting is always in the background, everything claustrophobic.

"This was a house *dying* for an audience," Kris writes, and in the first few seasons, that real-life audience was often older men. Joe Francis calls from jail to get the older sisters in a *Girls Gone Wild* swimsuit ad; Hugh Hefner convinces Kim to take off her clothes in a shoot for *Playboy*; Robin Antin of the Pussycat Dolls teaches Kim to pole dance on the first episode. It's a parade of raunch culture, and the shaky, uncomfortably close handheld shots in harshly lit suburban interiors recall the look of Y2K porn. In this sense, the house was of its time, a post-9/11 sexualized suburban fantasy: American flag pillows on the porch outside, stripper pole in the bedroom.

But this vibe doesn't last long. Season 4 gets some breathing room after Kris gets a new house, "a sprawling cream-colored Mediterranean-style house with a huge green front lawn—yet another dream house come true," she writes. (For security reasons, the exterior shown on the show is not the actual exterior of the house.) The Laura Ashley vibes are replaced with a kind of Z Gallerie-gone-wild take on Hollywood Regency, fit for the new queens of media. Kris renovates with the help of designer Jeff Andrews and turns nearly everything black and white, which creates high-contrast graphic pops on camera. By season 6, Kris puts down her famous checkerboard floor. By the twelfth season, the women's outfits are largely black and white, too.

The black-and-white world turns gray with the arrival of Kim's husband, Kanye West. The rapper and designer was a fan of minimalism before he married Kim (Italian architect Claudio Silvestrin designed his spartan New York apartment), and Kim and Ye hire Belgian designer Axel Vervoordt along with countrymate Vincent Van Duysen, Silvestrin, and the firm Family New York for their new Hidden Hills home. They keep the bones of an existing house, creating a weird McMansion wrapped in off-white plaster but set in a traditional suburban mowed-grass lawn. It's surreal, awkward, impractical. Pieces by the likes of modernist masters Jean Royère, Pierre Jeanneret, and Gerrit Rietveld populate the interior, and after Kanye removes the color, glitter, and glamour from his wife's closet, Kim begins wearing athleisure and sweats in shades of beige.

Kim and Ye's house becomes the family's new center of gravity, and its influence spreads: During one of Kris's seemingly unending renovations, Scott Disick, Kourtney's longtime boyfriend, remarks about how modernism is uncomfortably creeping into Kris's glossy

Regency home. "I'm almost allergic to how many different styles you have in this house," Disick tells Kris in season 12.

In this minimal greige era, the camera pulls back a bit more to create wider shots, facilitated by the fact that the homes are bigger, minimally furnished with oversize furniture like the sparsely decorated stage sets they are, leaving plenty of open space for sight lines. The scope widens conceptually as well, and in the to-camera "confessionals," the audience gets to see hair, makeup, and camera setups, a loose acknowledgment of the fourth wall. Instead of the cameras shakily intruding gonzo-style on the womens' lives, the show reveals more of its artifice. The women are now in control, no longer objects of attention but subjects sharing their home videos. As the fourth wall of the show falls, the domain of the show expands into the wider world. Kendall is a *Vogue* cover model. Kim is one of the most famous people in the world. Their homes—especially their kitchens—are no longer just less busy, they are almost unbelievably orderly. Khloé's perfectly organized glass cookie jars and pantry become something of a trademark. And the show's frenetic energy is largely gone, replaced by an uncanny stillness. Kim declares in the last season of *KUWTK*, "Calmness is my superpower."

That serenity extends to those watching. When high-stakes events unfold—break-ins, breakups—the audience already knows what's going to happen. The Kardashian-Jenners' lives have already been reported in tabloids, but on the show viewers get to see them more intimately and from the stars' perspectives. There's no uncertainty. A real-world marriage proposal is exciting but also scary—someone could say no—but when Ye proposes to Kim on the show, the audience knows that Kim will say yes. My friend Regina Bediako, a podcast producer, tells me that she sees the format as similar to unboxing videos or makeup tutorials on YouTube. As with those, the audience knows what the outcome will be, so the allure is not watching a drama reach an unforeseen conclusion but safely sharing someone's intimate emotional journey.

By now, the Kardashian-Jenners are far from zany. They are not shattered by overwork; they are powerful. Work is proof of their might. "I have the best advice for women in business," Kim controversially told *Variety* in 2022. "Get your fucking ass up and work." But architectural details aren't the only details erased in Kim's minimal era: The details of the actual work done to maintain these homes is gone, too.

"Every day, Latino people help create the illusion of the effortlessness of pampered whiteness," Héctor Tobar writes in the *Los Angeles Times* about the way service staff is kept out of sight across wealthy Southern California neighborhoods. The gardeners and housekeepers maintaining the Kardashian-Jenners' massive estates almost never appear on the shows, a rare exception being for a short clip in season 8 when Caitlyn enlists a housekeeper, Cruz, to play Ping-Pong. There's an uncanny sense that at the end of the day, everything is under control, and effortlessly so.

Americans have mythologized the frontier as the boundary between civilization, safety, and apple pie on one side and the yawning darkness where monsters wait to hatchet your children on the other. After almost twenty years on TV, the women have conquered the frontier of media and settled in. If the cluttered Cape Cod represented a desperate striving at the end of the Y2K raunch years, the Hollywood Regency era announced the arriviste media queens in the millennial Obama era, and the greige minimalism an otherworldly, vengeful superhero superstardom of Trump's first term, then the modern farmhouse telegraphs a sort of latter-day naturalism in the American colonial landscape.

—

In the 1990s, after decades of deindustrialization in Southern California, Barraclough tells me, the region experienced what some called the New White Flight, when many working-class and lower-middle-class white people lost their jobs, saw more immigrants arriving, and fled. White people migrated to rural areas across the country in an attempt to find a version of America where poverty, immigrants, and people of color didn't exist.

Wealthier whites didn't leave in the same numbers, though they also had access to rural fantasies closer to home in gated communities such as Hidden Hills. Kris moved her family behind the gates in 1996, and the idea that threatening forces lurk outside has been constant since the Kardashian-Jenner shows began.

Some of the threats shown on the show are physical and scary: Kylie is stalked, and a group of armed men tie up Kim and rob her in Paris. But these real and dangerous intrusions are blurred with the much less tangible threats that the family sees coming from a critical audience. After Kim is robbed, she talks about how people outside the family wonder if she faked the incident. Corey Gamble, Kris's boyfriend, tells Kim, "Anything you do, somebody will bring negativity and doubt to it . . . This family's gonna have to deal with that forever." In the next episode, Kim talks about people making light of the robbery online. "It just really sucks when you're getting judged by the whole world," she says.

And though people moved into gated communities such as Hidden Hills with the notion that these places would be safer than the denser, more diverse areas just down the freeway, Barraclough points out, "most crime occurs within communities . . . But it's always easier to imagine that the threat is outside, that it's a stranger. It's much harder to grapple with the reality that most violence and threats come from within our families and our social circles."

This is borne out in one of the central traumas that casts a long shadow over the show: Someone sells to the porn company Vivid a sex tape featuring Kim and her ex-boyfriend Ray J, she says, without her consent. But over the course of their shows, as the threats become more present, so does the stars' strength. Compare Kim discussing her sex tape leaking on the first episode of the E! show with her reaction to someone threatening to release extra footage from that tape in the first season of the Hulu show, fifteen years later. In 2007, Kim, in a pussy bow blouse, quietly explains to the camera that her privacy was violated and an intimate moment was publicly shared without her agreement. She seems to make herself small, her voice breathy and high, like a defendant pleading innocent on the stand. But in 2022, she responds full throatedly by telling lawyer Marty Singer, "I'm not going to let this happen to me again . . . I have all the time, all the money, and all of the resources to burn them all to the [bleeped] ground."

The Kardashian-Jenners have become pioneer women ready to take care of anyone who threatens them or their properties. Responses to threats become opportunities for shows of force, and there's a certain pleasure in being able to show force, presumably both for the people showing it and for the audience. And the more threats there are, the more opportunities to respond, creating a feedback loop. With every retaliatory salvo, the Kardashian-Jenners declare that they are no longer precarious, catering to the sexual desires of older men. At the same time, their show and its frontier mentality play into the country's pleasurable paranoia, obsessed with self-defense and standing one's ground, an America ready to blast a stranger just for knocking on its door.

The modern farmhouse represents a sort of optimism about self-reliance and stability. It's the frontier promise that things can be better if one goes it alone, or at least with only one's most trusted family.

That optimism is contagious, and that is what makes it dangerous. When our family isn't to be found, our surrogates on TV will have to do, always with us on our screens, giving us a shallow comfort while the depths of despair yawn beneath us. While the American pioneer dream may be working out okay for the Kardashian-Jenners, retreating for comfort into a fantasy of hard-working competitive isolation doesn't seem to be going that well for the rest of us.

"A relation of cruel optimism exists when something you desire is actually an obstacle to your flourishing," Lauren Berlant writes in *Cruel Optimism*. For the Kardashian audience, the cruelest optimism may not be people thinking that they too could be rich if they hustled harder, but that watching the show might do anything other than make people more docile and accepting of the country's competitive colonial obsessions.

A half century ago, during Southern California's pioneer revival era, the writer and futurist Alvin Toffler promoted the idea that new communication technologies would move production back into homes from factories and offices. In 1980 he published the best-selling book *The Third Wave*, in which he wrote that modern audiences and markets had been shattered into innumerable subcultures, each wanting something slightly different, and companies had begun offloading finishing touches to the consumer. He predicted the rise of people who were both producers and consumers—prosumers. Prosumers, he said, were already present in the rise of the do-it-yourselfers in the 1970s, and they seem alive today in anyone who uses social media, creating and consuming content at the same time.

"Once we recognize that much of our so-called leisure time is, in fact, spent producing goods and services for our own use—prosuming—then the old distinction between work and leisure falls apart," Toffler writes. "The question is not work versus leisure, but paid work . . . versus unpaid, self-directed, and self-monitored work."

In Toffler's eyes, homes were once again becoming sites of production, a return of sorts to preindustrial homesteading except now in "electronic cottages." Toffler seemed optimistic about the change. He saw it as a way past both communism and capitalism, which, like Borsodi, he saw as dependent on gargantuan industrial networks that dehumanized people and subsumed them in systems far beyond their control. Never mind that the divide between home and work was pretty much only a male thing for a long time—many women kept working at home, cooking, cleaning, and raising children, long after the Victorian age was a dusty memory. For Borsodi, the prosumer age promised to bring some agency back home, but it also, at least in the short term, seemed to benefit the owners of those large industrial systems because it required consumers to do production work for free. Prosumers are happy to do this because production is romanticized as expression, fun work akin to Borsodi raising his chickens. Only, now we are the chickens in our hybrid homes, alone with the pseudo-companionship of digital families, pushed into little cells so we can be controlled and used up. We're in farmhouse lofts, fattening ourselves up to be hung like trophies on a digital marketing executive's walls.

Today, the Kardashian-Jenners mostly seem happy in their electronic cottages—except for Kourtney. She's periodically dissatisfied with being on the show, accusing her sisters of faking their relationships with each other just so they have interactions to record, and she's tossed out the idea of quitting the show altogether. But so far she has stayed, trapped in the machine that keeps her rich and famous. She's unhappy, but we don't see her rage at the machine she's stuck in; she rages at her sisters for wanting to work with her. The machine doesn't rage at Kourtney for not working; her sisters rage at her instead. The work of regulation and punishment is outsourced to the subjects of the system, a prosumer fascism that promotes competition over cooperation. The Kardashian-Jenners are not freeing themselves in their electronic cottages. They are in control, their own bosses, only in the sense that their true boss is not a person but an economic system, the same system that everyone else in the country is beholden to, a system that stays resilient because it's often invisible.

Watching from our homes, we have even less agency. We're not even the farmers, just fat little chickens in our coops. And we're not just watching from our hybrid coops, we're reproducing the paranoia of our model farmers—or at least I am every time I find myself daydreaming about selling a business or book and making enough money to retire and disappear into some private castle. And though you may be noble-minded and untroubled by such fantasies, a quick turn through social media shows that there are plenty more people like me. Influencers and manosphere financial advisors the world over ape the Kardashian-Jenners, parlaying internet fame into brand deals and building a personal fortune big enough to retire on.

Part of the appeal of real estate shows like *Selling Sunset* may be that they show homes as places of work, aligning with what we, on some level, understand homes now to be. There's something soothing about watching people work in homes so efficiently.

The modern farmhouse trend won't last forever. It's already on the decline in Hidden Hills, De La Nuez reports, a victim of its own popularity. "Every house now along Valley Vista has become a modern farmhouse," he tells me in 2023. "We don't want to look like Valley Vista or Sherman Oaks or Encino."

Another faux-historical aesthetic may replace the modern farmhouse on HGTV, in Hidden Hills, and in Kris's and Khloé's lives, but the paranoid prosumer future will still be embedded in the country.

The United States is a colonial country, and the frontier period was an aggressively colonial one, when the nation was trying to manifest a new destiny by taking land across the continent away from the people who lived there and building new settlements in their place. As the Kardashian-Jenners show, the spirit of this era lives on, but what drove this spirit in the first place?

For white settlers, packing up and moving across a continent was dangerous. They could lose everything, including their lives, by separating themselves from the only land they had ever known and starting out somewhere new. Why risk it all?

Yes, the United States is driven by competition and work and money, but also by something even more foundational to our sense of self: love. Yearning for romance, Americans have reshaped the continent, building that feeling into millions of homes and establishing the abject misery that fosters dependency on hybrid homes today. Unfortunately, when it comes to destructive potential, love conquers all.

More romance than will ever be seen again on those sunny shores

Have you ever been on a trip and taken a deep breath while looking at the scenery before saying aloud to no one in particular, "This is a great place to fall in love"? I haven't either, but people do it on *The Bachelor* all the time. They rarely explain what they mean, and superficially these places—London, Budapest, Wisconsin—don't have much in common. But on the show, they're all destinations that contestants get to after sojourning at the Bachelor mansion, where the show now usually begins. A group of women start their competition to win the affections of a man by living together in this house before he selects a lucky few to jet around the world with him on a series of whirlwind dates in what are apparently supposed to be romantic locales. Arriving at the perfect place to fall in love requires first spending a few nights in a suburban, vaguely Mediterranean villa in the hills west of Los Angeles.

The mansion is one of the most enduring features of reality TV. *The Bachelor* and its companion show, *The Bachelorette*, have shot almost every season there since 2007. *Selling Sunset* has sold dozens of homes, *Real World* lofts have come and gone, and the Kardashians have cycled through estates, but the red-roofed house in Agoura Hills remains.

The mansion gives me the heebie-jeebies. It's not just that it's tinged with a Latin-lover exoticism; it has an uncanny appearance on the show, as though it's being remembered in a dream. It barely changes from season to season, frozen in an aged but eternal state. The stone flooring of the grand entry court where every contestant arrives is wet and glistening every evening despite the dry Southern California climate. Lights shining up from the ground turn scattered trees into shadows that rise into the dark sky. Blue lights glow out of the arches and portals in the facade as though it were a haunted house. Love, or something, is in the air.

The spectral atmosphere continues inside. The rose ceremonies, when the Bachelor decides who stays and leaves for that episode, take place at night among copious candles, sumptuous curtains, and more colored light oozing through elaborate grills. It all feels less Henry James and more *Phantom of the Opera*—a stage interpretation of European glamor for American masses who may never make it to Paris.

The mansion's Mediterranean Revival style is typical of modern suburbia across much of the southern and western parts of the United States, but the mansion, as it is inhabited on the show, is far from a typical suburban home. It may be a vehicle to marriage, but it's hardly a domestic idyll. It's a place for groups of men and women to bunk up and compete before either going back to where they came from or advancing on to the next phase of the game. It's a portal to a different life—an inferno for mid-level marketing managers to navigate with a middle-aged white guy as their Virgilian guide toward their one true love.

The home is as conceptually odd as the Mediterranean Revival style itself. With its elaborate courtyards and fountains and details pulled from Morocco, Tuscany, and southern Spain, the style is a kind of Orientalist fever dream that alludes more to Andalusian farmhouses than to anything built in the Americas before 1900, despite its modern ubiquity in the United States. It's so common in some places that it seems almost not worth paying attention to, a kind of ambient background architecture. It's a very strange thing that has become normalized, along with the contradictions it embodies.

American homes aren't all about conflict and competition. They're about seemingly gentler things, too: family, marriage, and kids and all that. But just as the Kardashian-Jenners show how spending time with surrogate sisters isn't all sweetness, *The Bachelor* and his home show the more sinister quality underneath even something as supposedly pure as falling in love.

The Bachelor Mansion is a permanent place of change, and it embodies a very strange relationship to land that millions of Americans take for granted—and, as I learned, it might not exist were it not for a book published almost 150 years ago.

"The Señora Moreno's house was one of the best specimens to be found in California of the representative house of the half barbaric, half elegant, wholly generous and free-handed life led there by Mexican men and women." This is the setting for the first half of Helen Hunt Jackson's hit 1884 novel, *Ramona*. "It was a picturesque life, with more of sentiment and gayety in it, more also that was truly dramatic, more romance, than will ever be seen again on those sunny shores . . . it can never be quite lost, so long as there is left standing one such house as the Señora Moreno's."

The book tells the tragic love story of Ramona, a child of Native American and Scottish parents raised as an aristocratic Mexican by Señora Moreno, a proud remnant of the Spanish landowning class left over after the United States' conquest of the American West in the Mexican-American War. Señora Moreno's house, set in the hills of Southern California, was part of one of the old ranchos that the Americans were taking for themselves.

"The Americans are running up and down everywhere seeking money, like dogs with their noses to the ground!" the Señora says, and throughout the book Anglo-American characters are usually violent and greedy, stealing property as fast as they can find it.

Ramona falls in love with Alessandro, a young Native American Luiseño man working at the Señora's house. In order to consummate their forbidden interracial romance, they flee to the countryside to try and make a life together in one of the Native American villages that Anglo settlers are quickly clearing so they can claim the land as their own. But the pair cannot escape the tragedy devastating their land and societies, and an Anglo eventually murders Alessandro. The couple's romantic demise captured the imaginations of readers. It's a romantic melodrama with star-crossed lovers that features the "wild" Southern California countryside, almost as though the moors of *Wuthering Heights* have been traded for the chaparral of the Southwest.

The book was an immediate sales success, but it was more than that. It became a cultural phenomenon.

Geographer Dydia DeLyser has described how tourists started flocking to places that supposedly inspired the book just a few years after it came out. Fans overwhelmed the residents of what readers decided was the "real" *Ramona* home with gawking, snooping, and souvenir-stealing. The supposed site of the couple's marriage became a destination that tourists visited alongside Yosemite and Mount Rushmore. Enterprising coattail-riders came out with Ramona water, beer, lemons, and more.

Ramona hit at a pivotal architectural time for the United States. At the end of the nineteenth century, the country was like an anxious teen figuring out who it was. A rise in domestic tourism led to voyages of self-discovery and an interest in histories and fictions that gave the nation's new body meaning. As the country adorned itself architecturally, it tried different styles. It had rebelled against its parental England and didn't want to look like that, but it didn't have another role model at hand. It had already done some neoclassical posturing, then went through a Gothic phase before dabbling in Italian fashions, but none of it was distinctly American.

The adolescent country was also going through a growth spurt. The United States started the nineteenth century as a rural nation and ended it as an urban one, but the roots of the suburban nation it would become were growing. Since the days of Thomas Jefferson, Americans had been romanticizing the positive effects of country life, and the affluent generally aspired to semirural homesteads where they could make their own private paradises. Toward the end of the century, large urban factories attracted immigrant labor and Black people from the rural South, and white reformers reacted with horror to the new conditions of city living. There was a moral panic about city life. The country was the cure.

Transportation innovations like railroads and streetcars spread scaffolding for sprawl.

Builders experimented with suburban developments of stand-alone single-family homes. Alexander Turney Stewart, developer of the U.S.'s first department store, planned Garden City, an innovative suburban development about twenty miles east of New York City on Long Island after the Civil War. John Kellum, the architect of 565 Broadway, shaped its plan. But such city planning innovations didn't answer the question of what the growing country's new homes should look like.

Construction innovations didn't help with that, either. Balloon-frame building was invented in the 1830s in the Midwest and spread across the country, and an adapted version of it is still how most American single-family homes are made. It uses standardized parts such as two-by-fours to create a structural framework that the building's skin attaches to. It's a flexible system that is simple to learn and easily incorporates a variety of finishes. If you've ever watched an HGTV show in which a contractor hammers through Sheetrock to expose the studs beneath, you've seen the essentials of the system. What was once was plaster lathe is now often plywood and gypsum board, but the basic idea remains the same.

Part of what makes balloon framing and similar systems so successful is that they can make houses that look like almost anything. Build a basic box, and you can tack whatever details you want on it; you can turn it into an ornate Tudor castle or keep it as austere as a Cape Cod saltbox.

This flexibility was an anomaly. Historically, how a building looked usually reflected how it was built. The elegant columns of Greece and Rome weren't just decorative—they were towers of marble that held up roofs. Elaborate traditional Chinese timber frames are skeletal mesh. Georgian facades are grids of structural brick. But the hidden bones of balloon-frame buildings could be covered in almost anything.

So what design to choose? Elizabethan and Queen Anne were popular home styles toward the end of the century, but as their name suggests, they looked to England, not America. Colonial Revival, the stylization of the East Coast homes of European settlers featuring white horizontal siding and a simple gabled roof, had more local roots and became popular—it still is today. But sunny Southern California, so far from the East Coast geographically and culturally, seemed to call for something different.

Señora Moreno's home suggested a way forward.

In her book *Ramona Memories*, DeLyser quotes Irving Gill, one of the most influential architects in Southern California in the early 20th century, who wrote: "Ramona's house, a landmark as familiar in the South as some of the Missions, was built around three sides of an open space . . . In California we have liberally borrowed this home plan, for it is hard to devise a better, cozier, more convenient or practical scheme for a home."

The model is essentially a U-shaped home around a central courtyard with covered outdoor spaces running along some walls.

"The house was of adobe, low, with a wide veranda on the three sides of the inner court, and a still broader one across the entire front, which looked to the south," Jackson writes in the novel. The sheltered outdoor spaces were particularly important. "The greater part of the family life went on in them. Nobody stayed inside the walls, except when it was necessary."

The machinations that drive the book's plot—the eavesdropping, passed notes, and sweet serenades between the star-crossed lovers—rely on the ease with which the home's rooms intermingle with the shared outdoor space. This romance could not have happened in a Queen Anne or any of the other popular Victorian styles with their agglomerations of compartmentalized spaces. Through the Señora's open house flowed possibility.

Along with the *Ramona* fever that swept Southern California in the 1880s, there was a more general interest in the architecture of the Spanish missions that dotted the state. In the 1890s, the influential journalist Charles Fletcher Lummis founded the Landmarks Club of California, which restored and promoted the largely rundown missions, an idea powerful admirers such as Harrison Grey Otis, the owner of the *Los Angeles Times*, took to. After the arrival of the Atchison, Topeka and Santa Fe Railway in Los Angeles in 1885, there was a rush of tourist and real estate investment, known as the Boom of the Eighties. Otis used *Ramona* and the missions to promote the region's allure. He moved into a mansion on Wilshire Boulevard inspired by the historic structures, in a style that would be called Mission Revival. The style took off, mostly in public buildings that were inspired by the relatively simple red tile–roofed missions and their light-baroque churches.

Architectural historian David Gebhard was the expert on the development of the Mediterranean Revival Style in Southern California. He marked the end of the early Mission Revival period around 1915, when it was superseded by the looser Mediterranean Revival Style, which blended vernacular Mexican, Spanish, Italian, and Moroccan elements. Plaster walls recalled adobe; exposed timber beams could've come out of the missions; glazed tile mimicked North Africa by way of Spain and Mexico. Decorative wrought iron, red tile roofs, and courtyards with elaborate fountains were uncommon back east but became practically required for the rich in SoCal. Anglo architects such as George Washington Smith, whose Montecito home designed in a sort of Andalusian farmhouse style was called "the germ of hope for future Californian architecture" in the magazine *Architectural Forum* in 1920, used a mélange of elements when designing high-end homes for new Anglo arrivals.

The Mediterranean Revival Style boomed in the 1920s, a heady decade when the teenage nation returned from the cataclysmic Great War shell-shocked but powerful, perhaps looking for new thrills to take the pain away.

"Evidences of the sordidness, the seriousness, the steadying business of life are all about us in woeful abundance; and we seek escape from the real world . . . into a world of dreams," wrote the architect Louis LaBeaume in a 1928 defense of "picturesque" building design against modernist criticism. He called for creations where "Hansel and Gretel, Red Olaf, Guy the Crusader, Don Quixote or Peleas and Melisande might be watching us from the windows."

Pop culture provided: Johnston McCulley's novel *The Curse of Capistrano* came out in 1919, and the next year it was adapted into the hit movie, *The Mark of Zorro*. The film launched a Marvel-esque franchise starring the masked Don Diego de la Vega pursuing the heart of his Lolita across Spanish California. In 1923, the town of Hemet began an annual outdoor performance of the *Ramona* play, which continues today. Another stage version starred Lawrence Griffith in the early 1900s; he went on to become director D. W. Griffith and made a movie version that premiered in 1910.

The landscape changed to match what was on stage and screen. The era's film stars such as Charlie Chaplin, Rudolph Valentino, and Mary Pickford moved into glamorous Spanish-style homes. In the 1920s and early '30s, the Mediterranean Revival Style became a default for Southern California in general. The red tile roofs were taking over.

"In the twentieth century American architectural scene, there has been only one brief period of time and only one restricted geographic area in which there existed anything approaching a unanimity of architectural form," Gebhard wrote. "This was the period, from approximately 1920 through the early 1930s, when the Spanish Colonial or the Mediterranean Revival was virtually the accepted norm in Southern California."

But the style didn't take over the country just by radiating out from the Southwest. It also grew out of somewhere even more fantastic—Florida—largely thanks to a man so colorful that Stephen Sondheim turned his life into a musical, though he is not very well remembered today.

In the words of early twentieth-century *New Yorker* writer Alva Johnston, Addison Mizner "was a blond giant, six feet two inches tall; he was fat but brawny. When he was approaching middle age and weighed two hundred and fifty pounds, he would startle social gatherings on Long Island by walking up and down the dance floor on his hands." For a time, he was a New York society fixture, known "as a big, breezy fellow who was usually accompanied by two handsome chows . . . Nearly everybody liked him."

Mizner grew up outside San Francisco in an affluent family. Though he wasn't especially bright, apparently, "he was an epidemic of good humor, radiating bonhomie," Johnston reports, which buoyed Mizner through a turbulent life. His appreciation for architecture kicked off after 1889, when President Harrison appointed his father envoy extraordinary and minister plenipotentiary to several Central American countries, and Addison moved to the region. Addison wrote of a stop in Mazatlan on Mexico's Pacific Coast on the way down, "It probably was the greatest day of my life, for there lying white in the sun was my first Spanish town."

Addison was able to see more Spanish towns when his family sent him to Salamanca to study in the hopes that he would become a better student, which didn't work out. After he returned he told his parents that he wanted to be an artist in a family of judges and diplomats, and they sent him to China to set him aright. He returned, Johnston reports, with a passion for Chinese art and fashion and several chow chows.

Mizner continued his almost unbelievable life back in San Francisco. The colorful character tried to prove his merit by working with prominent local architect Willis Polk, but Mizner blew through his money and left town to work in a gold mine. He eventually joined the Klondike rush in 1897, followed by a two-year trip around the Pacific and Indian Oceans.

Johnston writes:

In Hawaii, he did miniatures on ivory and made charcoal enlargements of photographs; in Samoa, he painted magic-lantern slides for a travelogue man; in Shanghai, he sold coffin handles to replace doorknobs; from Tokyo to Bangkok, he picked up commissions selling antiques; in Melbourne, he thrashed about the prize ring under the name of Whirlwind Watson; in Hawaii, he was fired from a job with the Inter-Island Steamship Company for nicknaming its ships "the Inter-Island pukers"; in Hawaii, also, he was created an extinct Polynesian nobleman by the deposed Queen Liliuokalani, who struck him with her royal yellow feathers and dubbed him Sir Addison as a reward for restoring the portraits of her ancestors.

While traveling, Mizner made money writing *The Cynic's Calendar* a joke book with twists on idioms, like "Where there's a will, there's a lawsuit." He rode his success back to San Francisco to become "the new Lumber King of the West" by marrying a timber heiress. Those plans fell through when she died unexpectedly, and the peripatetic bon vivant landed in New York, where "he made it a point of honor to live beyond his means," Johnston writes. At his Long Island home he installed kennels for dozens of chows and occupied himself designing homes for society friends in eclectic styles but didn't really commit to a career, and eventually in his mid-forties he had a sort of nervous breakdown and fled to Florida, finding his way to a restbed in Palm Beach.

It was there that Mizner's work really began and his flamboyant spirit took the physical form that would help transform the face of the country. He fell in with Paris Singer, one of the two dozen or so children of sewing-machine magnate Isaac Merritt Singer. Paris was also convalescing, and the two recovered by bonding over architecture and snobbery, apparently. After they healed, Singer hired Mizner to design the Everglades Club, an elitist Mediterranean Revival social club now known partially for its alleged racist entry policies. Its heyday coincided with the Florida Land Boom, one of the most feverish chapters of American real estate history.

Between its U.S. conquest and the 1920s, Florida had been a sleepy backwater for Anglos, inconvenient to reach for anyone outside it. In the early twentieth century, it began developing into a winter resort colony and sanatorium for wealthy convalescents such as Mizner and Singer, but after World War I, new railroads stretched across the Sunshine State, and the drip of interest in the area turned into a flood. Florida real estate became the base of a bubble that grew with seemingly no limits. Reports circulated of people making millions seemingly overnight; world royalty flocked to get in on the game. Johnston wrote that "the old rules for getting rich didn't apply to Florida."

Developers made up fake cities and geographical features to sell their new subdivisions. The "Berkshires of Florida" rose up miraculously out of the flat state in promotional brochures. Cities such as Miami shot up from almost nothing.

Mizner was the man for the moment. He would walk into a room with his chows, a monkey on one shoulder, a macaw on the other, and two larger monkeys in tow and win the best commissions in the state. The Everglades Club was his first calling card, and from there he conquered Palm Beach, designing homes for Vanderbilts and any other aristocrats looking to one-up the Joneses.

His signature style spread across the state: Coral Gables was built largely in Mediterranean Revival style with roof tile imported from Cuba, and for cereal heiress Marjorie Merriweather Post, architects Marion Sims Wyeth and Joseph Urban designed one of the country's grandest Mediterranean fantasies: Mar-a-Lago.

"Thus has California, and recently Florida, capitalized upon her history, romance and lore with the result that her architecture speaks more eloquently of her glorious present and colorful past than does any other phase of her artistic expression," architectural historian Rexford Newcomb rhapsodized in 1928 about the blossoming of the Mediterranean Revival style. "What California has done, what Florida, Texas, Arizona and New Mexico are doing, a well informed and artistically inclined profession may do for other areas of our country."

America was finding its style.

The design craze benefited from the country's auto boom in the 1920s. New highways led to new developments, and the popular styles spread wherever cars roamed. The first car-centric shopping center, Country Club Plaza in Kansas City, opened in 1923 in a Mediterranean Revival Style with a replica of the Giralda Tower—once a minaret of the Great Mosque—of Seville.

And the style might have taken over the whole country had the roaring twenties lasted longer, but everything changed in the '30s. The Great Depression was not a time for decadence, and the curlicues and glittering tiles of Mediterranean Revival became passé. The popping of the Florida real estate bubble destroyed Mizner financially; he died in debt in '33. Nationally, civilian housing construction slowed during the Depression and nearly halted during World War II. Afterward, the style was superseded by designs more aligned with the practical concerns of an ascendant middle class and an interest in modernism that pooh-poohed historical inclinations.

Johnston wrote that Lillias Piper, a high-society interior decorator who worked with Mizner, called him "the Hans Christian Andersen of architects," creating storybook confections that were stage sets for myths and legends. Though the magic seeds for it had been planted, the Bachelor Mansion would have to wait.

—

After the war, suburban construction roared. It took a few years after 1945 for the building industry to kick into high gear, but after so many years without much activity, there was enormous pent-up demand, and government policy funneled it into suburbs.

By 1950, US suburbs were booming, growing much faster than the country's cities. This new housing era was guided less by affluent dreams and pseudo-historical world-building and more by the mechanics of federal bureaucracy and a triumphant economy. Thanks to policies such as the 1934 Housing Act, which created the Federal Housing Administration (FHA) and the basis of the modern American mortgage insurance system, it was often effectively cheaper for white Americans to buy a home than to rent one. The suburban single-family freestanding home became a model of the independent family units that made up the new superpower.

The financial guarantees created by the FHA were not just invisible strings of bureaucracy; they had a massive effect on what postwar suburbs looked like. In the 1920s, developers would typically buy a tract of land and lay out a neighborhood and then sell plots to builders, who would decide on the style and form of the new homes. Developments could end up with a mix of styles, especially if builders competed to outdo their neighbors. In the '50s, however, developers were backed by federal mortgage guarantees and frequently could raise capital not only to buy the land for a development but to build the houses on it, too. Developers didn't invest in design diversity. A copy-and-paste mentality led to thousands of nearly identical homes in a single development. Postwar suburbs such as Levittown were filled with small houses that looked almost exactly the same. No courtyard fountains, no grand porticos.

Architectural historian James A. Jacobs writes in *Detached America* that the average square footage of new houses fell from 1,177 in 1940 to 983 during the first half of the '50s as developers scrambled to build cheap starter homes to satisfy the pent-up demand created by the Depression and World War II construction stoppages. Homes often fell to the minimum standards required to get FHA backing, so "unnecessary" features such as porches disappeared. FHA evaluators favored Cape Cod and other styles that produced basic boxes with gabled roofs and few other details for their apparent economy. Thanks to national developers, those styles spread like kudzu.

But the boom didn't last long. Even by the end of the Korean War in the mid-'50s, the housing market had started to change. After the starter home market was satiated, builders needed a new product to sell. This era pioneered the concept of planned obsolescence in consumer products, and builders had their own version of this, regularly releasing new designs with the latest built-in gadgets and *Jetsons*-esque design features such as built-in vacuums or intercoms. Split-level homes expanded the modest dimensions of their first-generation postwar predecessors. These were upgrade homes for repeat buyers—iHomes of sorts—and they kept the American suburban revolution alive.

Between 1950 and 1970, most of the country's population growth was in its suburbs. The suburban ranch style flourished in this period. With a single story under a long, low roof, it could seem more spacious than the first wave of postwar suburban housing, but it was simple enough to be relatively cheap to build at scale. Though it originally borrowed from Spanish colonial haciendas, which were working ranch buildings, postwar architects such as Cliff May abstracted architectural references enough for the style to wander free of any associations to a specific place. Ranch-style homes ditched red tile roofs for asphalt shingles. Ranches showed up across the country and helped erode regional variations in suburban styles. Everything started to look the same.

Ranch homes were modern. They had sliding glass doors, big windows, and open interiors. Mediterranean Revival dreamed of a fantastic past; ranch style looked to an easy future. It was an optimistic style for an atomic-age country believing its best days were ahead and that the grass was greener behind a tract home. By 1970, the United States was the world's first suburban civilization, and much of it was ranch country.

Then, once again, things changed. The Fair Housing Act of 1968 had chipped away at segregation and the notion that suburbs were refuges for racist white people, and inflation and rising housing costs put new homes increasingly out of reach. Between '74 and '80, the average house price almost doubled. Condo ownership was also legalized in all fifty states in '68, and social change meant there were more double-income households, single-person households, and woman-led households. The dominance of the suburban single-income nuclear family home waned.

Styles changed, too. The vision of modern progress manifested in shiny new gadgets and white male hegemony was falling apart. Dreams from the past returned. Postmodern architecture embraced history. Mediterranean Revival resurged, a bit of nostalgia when the idea of the future was losing its luster. And now it wasn't just for the homes of the rich and famous. The red tile tide, as the architectural historian Aaron Betsky called it, covered gas stations, fast food stands, university buildings, city halls—everything in swaths of the country from Sacramento to Fort Lauderdale.

This was the same period when loft living was becoming cool. Cities, once old and smoky and run by industry, were on their way to becoming shiny and new again in the gloss of the digital age. The suburbs were becoming something else.

After the inflation of the 1970s subsided, houses grew again in the '80s, this time without any futurist aspirations for suburbia of the postwar period. Spaces started to mutate: double-height foyers, opulent primary suites, luxurious walk-in closets. The McMansion was born, and architects embraced the red tile style. By the '90s, the Mediterranean Revival style often appeared under the "Tuscan" label. Tuscan kitchens popped up in McMansions, and magazines dedicated to "Tuscan" home design thrived, but the Tuscan Revival homes resembled their American Mediterranean Revival counterparts more than the houses you might find in the hills outside Florence. But throughout the twentieth century, Anglo Americans demonized people from Spanish-speaking cultures. The creep in real estate terminology from Spanish Colonial to Mediterranean to Tuscan Revival probably has as much to do with ethnic anxieties as with architectural developments.

As the contemporary Mediterranean Revival architect Marc Appleton has noted, Anglos had also seen Europe's boot in California since the days of Henry James, who called the state "a sort of prepared but unconscious and inexperienced Italy." Italian gardens were particularly popular in the late nineteenth and early twentieth-century Mission Revival days; Edith Wharton published *Italian Villas and Their Gardens*, a design guide-cum-travelogue, in 1904. George Washington Smith, the architect who helped popularize Mediterranean Revival in California, based a house he designed on the Florentine Villa Gamberaia, one of those covered by Wharton in her book. A Tuscan influence had arguably permeated the Mediterranean Revival style since the start of the twentieth century.

And at the end of the twentieth century, the red tile tide crept its way up the highlands dividing Los Angeles and the San Fernando Valley to a newly incorporated city called Agoura Hills. There, Marshall and Joanna Haraden built and designed a 7,500-square-foot home, which was completed in 2005. They named it Villa de la Vina. It debuted on *The Bachelor* just two years later.

Red tile roofs had been sheltering American romances since their first "revival." During their second, they took the fantasy prime time.

The Bachelor premiered in March 2002. It originally shot in a different location, a Malibu beach house that was a quasi-modernist take on Mediterranean Revival: It had white walls and unornamented windows, but also a red tile roof and grand entry court where the Bachelor met the contestants. But since 2007 almost every season of the *The Bachelor* and *The Bachelorette* has shot at Villa de la Vina. Even when scheduling conflicts get in the way, the production team tends to find alternate locations that mimic the Villa, as it did for the 2024 season of *The Bachelorette*, which took place in a stylistically close cousin. Mediterranean Revival is integral to the show.

The show's sumptuous styling distinguishes it from raunchier peers such as *Temptation Island*, in which couples test their relationships by living in houses with scantily clad temptations. *The Bachelor* features suits and sparkly cocktail dresses, plus candles, roses, and the mansion. Although Mediterranean Revival had trickled down to fast-food chains and rented condos, it still had its origins as an aspirational style. It was invented for rich people, and it lends the show a sheen that has endured through the show's many problems.

The show's visual style has "just enough fantasy element to where it's not totally insane-looking," Angelic Rutherford, the longtime production designer for *The Bachelor, The Bachelorette*, and their many spinoffs, tells me. "Our show has to feel and look natural but also be in this fantasy world, you know?"

It's a fantasy world of Victorian love and romance that owes a lot to another fantasy world that's a little more lurid.

In the 1990s, cheaper recording equipment and online distribution meant videos could be made almost anywhere by anyone, and personal computers meant they could be shared between homes around the world. One type of video in particular took off. Amateur porn and porn that promised to show what "regular" people would do on-screen—what the artist Sergio Messina calls "realcore"—flourished. Celebrity sex tapes, leaked or stolen, became a sort of craze, ranging from Pamela Anderson and Tommy Lee's in 1995 to Ray J and Kim Kardashian's in 2007.

Y2K reality TV and porn often shared an aesthetic: handheld cameras invade personal space, jostling and bouncing around their subjects, coming closer to flesh than sitcom lenses ever did, denying their subjects any boundaries. Or sometimes static CCTV-esque cameras surveil unblinkingly, eliminating any sense of privacy or control.

Porn may even have been a forebear to reality TV—at least one porn-maker seems to think so.

"I created reality television," Joe Francis, the creator of *Girls Gone Wild*, told journalist Scaachi Koul in 2023. Francis started *Girls Gone Wild* in 1997, selling videos of young women talked into taking off their clothes and more, often on spring break at the shore. "It turned me on to see these girls on spring break because it was reality."

Girls Gone Wild and its ubiquitous TV ads defined the contradictions of the late '90s that incubated reality TV. This was the raunch era, when sexuality fed the nation's anxiety. The remains of the postwar fantasy of the Victorian nuclear family were disintegrating. The emptiness of its promise was starting to show, and the social structure underpinning the most powerful political entity the world had ever known was crumbling. People were delaying marriage and having fewer children. The United States had the highest rate of divorce of any wealthy nation in the early '90s, and lawmakers tried to bolster the wobbling institution by excluding people from it: In 1996 Congress passed the Defense of Marriage Act, which defined marriage as only being between a man and woman under federal law, and in the early 2000s legislators pursued a federal constitutional amendment against gay marriage. The conservative impulse to "protect" marriage overlapped with the conservative impulse to exploit women sexually on camera, different manifestations of the desire to exploit women generally at a time when more women were succeeding professionally and economically.

At the same time, the idea of work was changing in the United States, thanks to the neoliberal era that the Reagan years and the Clintonian Democrats had ushered in. Unions were weakened, workers' solidarity a notion of yesteryear, and individuals prowled the marketplace, competing to get work and survive. The early reality competition shows made the competition of capitalist life explicit, and a subsequent wave of shows pushed further into dystopia in a slightly different direction than the Kardashians did.

American Idol came out in June 2002 and was the highest-rated show on television from 2005 through 2011. Shows such as *America's Next Top Model* followed, extending the format to other fields. The winners of such shows usually don't go on to massive success in their careers and often fade into obscurity despite performing the "best" among their cohort.

On these shows labor is not sweaty drudgework to ensure survival; it's creative, a matter of artistry and skill, and the most talented and committed contestants win. On *Survivor* and *Big Brother*, contestants often speak approvingly of an opponent's gameplay even if it includes a bit of deception and subterfuge—game recognizes game—but the talent shows are nobler meritocracies. Generally, villains here don't win, and the top spot goes to someone virtuous and admirable who "deserves" to succeed. On these shows, people love to work, and it is an honor to have the opportunity to model, design clothes, or style hair. Karl Marx wrote about capitalist society alienating laborers from their labor, detaching a sense of identity from one's occupation or the product of their work, turning people into anonymous workers punching the clock at the discretion of their bosses. Talent competition shows depict fantasies of de-alienated labor, where identity and work intertwine and result in glorious performance.

The two threads of work and sexuality come together in *The Bachelor*. It is, superficially, a dating game show. Those had been around for decades by the time *The Bachelor* premiered: *The Dating Game* began in 1965 and ran for years on ABC. It featured a few contestants competing for dates, with new groups introduced on nearly every episode. But *The Bachelor* is different, formatted more like contemporaneous talent competitions than anything else.

The Bachelor premiered in March 2002, a bridge moment between the tropical raunch of *Girls Gone Wild* and the competition of *American Idol*. Like the former, it featured young white women drinking and performing for male attention; like the latter, it created a supposedly meritocratic tournament in which a judge (the Bachelor) decides who is most worthy of winning. The women's talent is their suitability for marriage. Contestants with hidden agendas are villains; virtuous believers in the game of love are heroes. Dating becomes a form of competitive work. Any *Bachelor* contestant suspected of being on the show just to get famous is there "for the wrong reasons." One must not be alienated from the primary job at hand: the labor of love.

The Bachelor has lasted longer than its soft-core predecessor. *Girls Gone Wild* pioneered a mix of performance, exploitation, and "reality," but ultimately it came and went with peak Y2K raunch culture. The company eventually went bankrupt, and Francis sold his stake to another porn brand. But *The Bachelor*'s more valorous mix of suburban sexuality, romance, and competition lives on.

There was, strangely, something forward-thinking, or at least innovative, about the show, similar to how the Mediterranean Revival architectural style isn't a recreation of the past but a repackaging of bits and pieces from here and there to create something new.

Despite its conservative trappings vaunting monogamy, heterosexual marriage, and restrictive gender roles, *The Bachelor* isn't manifesting some traditional past, either. The setup is hardly the picture of domesticity in any era. In its residential setup, the show has more in common with *The Girls Next Door*, the 2000s reality show that followed Hugh Hefner's girlfriends living in the Playboy Mansion, than any postwar sitcom or Victorian novel.

But even the nineteenth-century ideal of a man and woman wedding and creating a nuclear family in a home of their own with no other activity or extended family in it is a contrivance. The notion was a Western reaction to the schism of home and male labor created by industrialization, which pulled artisans out of home workshops and into factories with sweaty homosocial settings. Heterosexual nuclear family domestic bliss is as modern a creation as the word *heterosexual* or the phrase *nuclear family*.

The American suburban single-family home is an invented "traditional" idea. From that perspective, Mediterranean Revival is the perfect contemporary style for it. The post-1970s Mediterranean Revival is a revival of a "revival" of a style that never really existed. There never was a "Mediterranean style" to revive in the first place; it's an amalgamation of references combined to create an ersatz idea of history dreamed up by the likes of Addison Mizner.

The Bachelor, however, *is* now a relic of an earlier age, not from some traditional past but from the paternalistic early 2000s raunch era that spawned it. *The Bachelor* and *Bachelorette* were something close to whites-only club for years; the former had its first Black lead in 2021, in its twenty-fifth season. For years, a white man named Chris Harrison oversaw the proceedings as the show's host, often scolding women who somehow stepped out of line, and he left the show only after he seemed to defend Rachael Kirkconnell, a white former *Bachelor* contestant, when photos emerged online of her at an antebellum plantation-themed fraternity party.

In a 2021 conversation with Rachel Lindsay, the first Black Bachelorette, for the entertainment news show *Extra*, Harrison seemed to chide Lindsay when she said that attending an "Old South antebellum party" is "not a good look." "Well, Rachel," he responded, "is it a good look in 2018, or is it not a good look in 2021?" "It's not a good look ever," she says. He then lectures Lindsay about how common such parties were in 2018. He stepped away from the Bachelor shows later that week and was eventually replaced by former *Bachelor* contestant and NFL quarterback Jesse Palmer.

Even *The Bachelorette*, which potentially gives its sole female contestant more power as she chooses between her suitors, has the paternalist host and maintains the focus on marriage. When the Bachelorette chooses her final winner, her man still takes the symbolic action, getting down on one knee and proposing to her.

Newer dating shows have tried to ditch some of *The Bachelor* and its siblings' baggage: *Love Is Blind* presents itself as a noble experiment in overcoming beauty norms; *Are You the One?* featured a mixed-gender queer season where everyone in the cast was open to dating anyone else in the cast; *Couple to Throuple* ditches monogamy altogether, focusing on three-way relationships. Even cheekier shows such as *MILF Manor* or *For the Love of DILFs*, which feature intergenerational relationships, maintain a lighter tone, avoiding the past-midnight drunken emotional breakdowns that were a mainstay of *The Bachelor*.

The Bachelor remains one of the more "traditional" dating shows—it's not *Love Island*, which features racially diverse groups of men and women mixing and mingling with nary a mention of marriage. In the mansion, the dream of the perfect love persists. And audiences still watch Bachelors wed their Bachelorettes while swiping through dating apps on their couches.

The fantasy of finding one true love endures not because romance has proven its worth. It has more to do with the competition shows that helped spawn *The Bachelor* and the neoliberal lifestyles they represent. In gig economies or any industry without strong unions, free agents jump through the air with minimal safety nets, looking for someone to catch them before they crash. People live in competitive isolation, moving away from the places they were born and the people who raised them, looking for opportunities in communities that don't know them, led by governments that leave them to fend for themselves. People fantasize about finding someone who will stick around for a lifetime when no one else will.

Historian Catherine Gudis has described an "aesthetic of amnesia" running through the red tile style that forgets the brutality of the Spanish missions, where colonizers tore apart Native American families, brutalized women with sexual violence, imposed a new language and religion, and carried out cultural genocide. Anglos probably wanted to ignore all this when they moved to California and the Southwest. Copying the old Spanish and Mission styles too exactly may have made it harder to forget the past. Revising the pig of history, cutting out the unsavory bits, and remixing the rest to create some wonderful new synthetic meat is tempting, but the result is still baloney.

—

One last detour on the *Bachelor* journey: In the early twentieth century, New York architect Bertram Goodhue embraced an elaborate style of Spanish Baroque architecture called Churrigueresque. He learned about the style on a trip to Mexico, which he documented in a published journal. On his trip through what he called the "Egypt of the New World," he admired local wonders.

"They never employ an architect for such buildings as these," he wrote of humble Mexican structures, whose creators "seem to have just that innate sense of what goes to make true beauty." On his trip, he spent a lot of time admiring the local women, too. "What names they have! Couldn't you love a Mercedes, or a Dolores, or an Inez more readily than Annie or a Susan?" There's no mention of a Ramona, but he wrote, "The Indian girls of Mexico are all fair—yes, all! And those who are not, pardon the paradox, are certain to possess an expression of the eyes, or maybe but a soft hollow in the nape of their neck, which is absorbingly interesting."

Goodhue's lust suffused his experience of space: "Take a stroll around the Zocalo, or beneath the trees of the Alameda of an evening, and if your dreams are untroubled afterward you may as well return from whence you came, for none of the romance of the land can you appreciate." He concluded with a story of his impossible romance with Dolores, a local young woman. She supposedly told him "although you are an 'estrangero,' you are 'muy caballeroso.'" In the end, she came to see the architect off, "almost whispering, 'Adios, Beltran; vaya usted con Dios.'"

In *Ramona Memories*, DeLyser cites the historian T. J. Jackson Lears, who wrote about a sense of "weightlessness" among Victorian Americans, who "wandered through the Unreal City," Lears wrote, adrift in the new rationalist, industrial society. Rapid, destabilizing urbanization led many to seek experiences that were more "real" than their daily lives, and many retreated into nostalgia. Hordes of *Ramona* readers sought the "real" people and places from the book, though Jackson never identified any. Two possible real Ramona homes popped up; even a real Ramona and Alessando. Charles Fletcher Lummis, the Anglo journalist who started the Landmarks Club, became so enamored of California's Spanish colonial past that he called himself Don Carlos and tried to marry into the del Valles, the prominent family that owned one of the supposed models for the Señora's home in *Ramona*.

Goodhue brought Churrigueresque architecture back to California; he designed much of the Panama–California Exposition, a sort of world's fair held in San Diego's Balboa Park in 1915 and '16. Millions came to it, and its fantastical architecture became a sensation. Churrigueresque is ornate even by Baroque standards—wriggling columns and towers covered completely in sculptures, ornamentation everywhere. The popularity of this work helped move the Mission Revival craze into its more broadly influenced Mediterranean era as the differing styles melded together.

Goodhue brought the romance of his travels home, seeming to believe that romance was endemic to Mexico and its architecture and not his exoticizing gaze. It felt good to be the "gentlemanly stranger," and he built the architecture of that experience into the landscape of the United States. The heavy romance of the fantasy felt more real than the weightlessness of industrializing America.

The *Bachelor* mansion is not the site of the domestic bliss enjoyed by a nuclear family. It is the waystation that begins a journey to the perfect place to fall in love and then head off elsewhere. This site of change is what has endured so long on TV. The mansion wouldn't be remarkable if it were an exceptional place, like Disneyland, that people visit and then leave to return to their "real" lives. It would be just another stage set. But the mansion is like thousands of other homes across the country. It's part of the stage where millions of Americans perform their daily lives, where they create their fantasies and pursue their loves with the conviction of a method actor that they are living their "reality" and not just following scripts that white men wrote for them 150 years ago.

Helen Hunt Jackson didn't want *Ramona* just to be a love story for the ages or enthrall people with the spell of a romanticized past. She wanted to help people. Inspired by how Harriet Beecher Stowe galvanized white

Americans against slavery with *Uncle Tom's Cabin*, she wanted to open the eyes of Americans to what their country was doing to Native Americans. "If I can do one hundredth part for the Indian that Mrs. Stowe did for the Negro, I will be thankful," she wrote.

In Riverside, not far from where *Ramona* was set, Anglos built the Sherman Institute, a boarding school where young Native American students were ripped from their culture and forced to adopt the lifestyles of their oppressors. It had five buildings in the Spanish Colonial Revival style built by Native American laborers. There was even a building named for Ramona.

The colonial love myth is baked into the physical fabric of the country. Even well-intentioned colonists get twisted by the search for new reality that drives people to conquer new land. Jackson, with all her hopes of helping Native Americans, still has her narrator describe Mexican life as "half barbaric," though it's not meant to be a bad thing. It's the lead-in to describing Mexican life as "half elegant, wholly generous and free-handed." The barbarism is an asset for a bourgeois Victorian, desiccated by a life shaped by impersonal economic systems. A barbaric life is brutal and real. It's shaped by powerful physical feelings: the heat of the sun, the bite of the cold, the sting of violence. These are forces that Ramona and Alessandro have to endure in their romantic flight through the wilderness. They leave civilization and get to enjoy reality. This is what Victorians wanted from this kind of realist fiction, what Goodhue wanted from Mexican architecture, what fans of *Ramona* wanted to find in Southern California, what we want from our hybrid homes today.

The United States has spent decades blanketing its land with homes for isolated nuclear families looking to escape into lives that are more "real." American homes keep people feeling lacking while promising to fill the voids they create, and the holes go deeper than pits of wealth, down to love and marriage and very deep emotional senses of being.

Jacobs quotes Russell Lynes, of the brow chart, who wrote in 1963 about the American attitude toward home: "To many an American the ideal house is a disposable house like the log cabin—warm and comfortable while he is in it, but easily got rid of when opportunity or whim or tragedy beckons him to move on." The modern suburban home is a beacon to the next adventure, the next attempt at a meaningful life, true happiness, starting over, but the next home is just another disappointing fantasy. We have now rebuilt our physical landscapes in the image of these fantasies, and their lonely disappointments are driving us into the arms of Real Worlders and Kardashians and whoever else is on our screens, making us crave the digital homes and their delirious effects.

Anglos in America have been chasing mirages since John Winthrop dreamed of building a city on a hill. It's the land of opportunity, hope, change, not stability. Which could be harmless enough, bad for the lunatic dreamers if no one else, if constant escaping didn't require someone else's land to escape to, some new California to claim, some perfect place to fall in fantastic love and erase whatever actual relations had been there.

DeLyser notes that in *Ramona*, it's the Anglos and Spanish Mexicans who meet happy ends. Native Americans, she writes, have no romantic escape.

During the early days of the *Ramona* craze, a Native American Cahuilla woman named Ramona Lubo often posed as the real Ramona. Like the character in the book, her husband had been murdered by Anglos, and tourists took pictures with her, though they were disappointed that she didn't look or act like they wanted—she wasn't a fair-skinned young woman singing *rancheras* by the fire. After she died, she was buried beneath the fiction created on top of her. Next to her husband's grave—marked with both his real name, Juan Diego, and Alessandro—DeLyser finds her plot simply labeled "Ramona." And she was still being devoured by fiction long after she was gone. In 1973, the Cahuilla Tribe cut off public access to the cemetery with the graves because visitors were taking away bits of the site for souvenirs. The power of love.

You act like I have a new face or something

A few minutes into the premiere of the sixth and final season of *The Hills*, a black Suburban drives up to a chalet-style home with a wreath on the front door on a snowy day. "Crested Butte, Colorado," the title on the screen says. Heidi Montag's parents' house. Then there's an interior shot of a bookshelf—one book by Anne Lamott, *When Mothers Pray* by Cheri Fuller—and a photo of young Heidi behind them. The doorbell rings, and the scene shifts to a shot of Darlene, Heidi's mother, greeting her daughter at the door, Heidi's back to the camera.

"I knew you were gonna cry," Heidi says. "Oh, it's so nice to be home."

This is the beginning of a breakthrough moment not only for reality TV but for the United States overall.

The camera still doesn't show Heidi from the front and instead shows more framed snapshots of the family before Heidi sits with her mom on a couch and her visage finally appears on-screen.

"What, you act like I have a new face or something," Heidi says with a hint of a smirk on her otherwise immobilized features.

Heidi's being ironic. She does indeed have a new face, the product of a barrage of cosmetic procedures that had been publicized in the months leading up to the episode airing. The audience has tuned in to see the big reveal, which her mother was experiencing in person. This was before the storylines on the Kardashians rehashed what people had already read in the tabloids. Heidi was pioneering how reality TV could turn old news into melodrama, eroding any distance between entertainment and fact.

"It takes a little getting used to," Darlene says, looking at her daughter. "Are you happy?" she asks, to which Heidi responds that she's feeling a lot better. "What all did you have done?" Darlene asks, and Heidi answers: "I got a slight eyebrow lift, and that's why I had these staples in my head . . . I had my nose redone. I had my own fat injected into my cheeks. I had my ears pinned back. I had injections in my lips. I had my chin shaved down. I had my breasts redone and my back shaped. And then I had a little bit of inner and outer lipo done."

Darlene tells Heidi that she risked her life to have these elective procedures. "I just feel like that when you left home, you had more confidence and more self-esteem than any person I'd ever met in my life," Darlene says. Heidi responds by saying that she's toyed with modifying her body since she was young and that she has "always wanted big boobs." She says she wanted even bigger implants, but they wouldn't fit.

It's no surprise that this conversation is about a body, takes place in a home, and is between family members. Homes are safe spaces where the most intimate private truths can be discussed by the people who hold each other most dear. Your family and your body are the last things you have left when everything is stripped away. But Heidi showing everything that she did to change her body makes her mother uneasy along with everyone in the audience. She has changed her fundamental truths. She is not as real as she appears to be.

"It sounds to me like you wanna look like Barbie," Darlene says.

"I do wanna look like Barbie."

"Nobody in the world could have looked like Heidi Montag," Darlene says.

Now Heidi doesn't even look like Heidi. Some new entity has taken her place.

"Are you telling me you don't think I look good?" Heidi asks.

"Maybe you should rephrase the question."

Heidi persists.

"I thought you were more beautiful before," Darlene says before the scene ends with Heidi in tears.

A makeover typically makes someone better than they were before. In Darlene's eyes, Heidi's makeover was a failure, or something worse: the loss of her daughter to the pressures of reality TV.

Heidi doesn't make it through that season of the show. A rift grows between her and her friends and sister in Los Angeles, one arguably created by her new husband, Spencer Pratt. He is alternatively aggressive and indolent on the show, apparently unemployed, sequestered in their modernist hillside home, and resentful of anyone who takes his wife's time away from him.

"The only thing Heidi does is read and write poetry and pray and read books," Spencer tells their friend, Kristin Cavallari. "I don't let her go on TV, no computers."

Spencer becomes seemingly paranoid and erratic, obsessed with the healing power of crystals to the point that his friends begin to find him odd. "These people don't know how [bleeped] dangerous I am," he says at a nightclub, where he shows up emotional and gets in a fight with his friends.

Heidi stands by her man. "Spencer didn't change me," she tells Cavallari. "I changed myself."

Heidi is the empowered frontier woman, setting off from her parents' Colorado lodge to reinvent everything about herself out west with a wild man.

For this, she was the villain. Eventually Heidi's sister, Holly, gathers with the other women on the show, and they mourn Heidi's transformation and decide to cut the couple off. "So, we'll just stop talking about them, all of us," Stephanie Pratt, Spencer's sister, says. Holly delivers the closing remarks. "I just feel like she's gone forever," she says before sobbing.

Since the beginning of *The Hills*, Heidi was the foil to Lauren Conrad. Like Becky Sharp, the willful, wicked lead of William Makepeace Thackeray's *Vanity Fair*, Heidi rolled her eyes at her dutiful counterpart. The show starts with Lauren and Heidi enrolling at the Fashion Institute of Design and Merchandising, and Heidi skips class on her first day. She'd much rather get into the working world immediately and scores her dream job at a public relations and event planning company, but she's soon bored of that, too, glumly staring at her work computer calendar showing "9:00 a.m.: Start work, 6:00 p.m.: Finish work" repeated endlessly.

Heidi is unlike Lauren, who strives for *Teen Vogue* internships in Paris and New York, and even less like Lauren's intern rival, Emily Weiss, who would go on to found the billion-dollar beauty brand Glossier and become an emblem of girlboss feminism.

Heidi was bound for something different. While on *The Hills*, she landed magazine covers and released music. She and Spencer published a book, *How to Be Famous: Our Guide to Looking the Part, Playing the Press, and Becoming a Tabloid Fixture*, with a cover mimicking a celebrity gossip magazine. They appeared on the second season of the *Survivor*-esque reality series *I'm a Celebrity... Get Me Out of Here!* Heidi was an influencer before there were influencers, bravely making money for having a kind of recognizable name when people said she shouldn't.

In 2010, on an episode of ABC's *Nightline* she sits down for an interview with journalist Juju Chang to discuss her surgeries and her career.

"A lot of people think this is what's wrong with American culture is precisely what you said, that you think it's an honor to be famous for being famous," Chang says.

"I'd rather be getting a paycheck for being famous for being famous than working at my parents' restaurant," Heidi says.

"But I would argue that there's virtue in the hard work," Chang says. "I would rather work at the restaurant."

"But that would be *your* path," Heidi says, unbent.

After *The Hills,* Heidi released more music and appeared with Spencer on other reality shows, such as *Celebrity Big Brother* and *Celebrity Wife Swap,* but she never matched the level of fame that the MTV show brought her. Her star rose too soon. Along with Spencer, she was one of reality TV's first great villains, creating a name for herself by being unvirtuous in the eyes of commentators such as Chang and winning an audience in the process. But she suffered in the earnest millennial era with its faith in America's meritocratic myth, that by working hard in a service job, maybe at your parent's restaurant, you could get ahead.

She wasn't an outcast just because she didn't want to work in a restaurant, though. She was seen as evil because, as she was quick to point out across her body, she was "fake." She was a sellout and a phony when those accusations still mattered. But her crime was just doing what Adam DiVello, *The Hills*'s creator, had been doing so successfully: taking advantage of Americans' faith in video to portray reality to create a new reality for herself.

Heidi was a harbinger of the literally cutthroat times to come, when *Real Housewives* would return every season with a face changed by a neck lift to be celebrated for their ability to change themselves to suit the game they're playing. Had she arrived a few years later, Heidi's reception would have been very different. She was too early to benefit from the future she helped create.

As the 2010s went on, the machinations of reality shows became repetitive and transparent. The novelty had worn off. Americans got used to seeing how reality was rigged on and off their screens and started to root not for the canned hero ordained by invisible higher forces but for the wicked one winking through the screen, saying, "Let's have some fun." As 2016 approached and Donald Trump announced his candidacy for president, America was rooting for the villain.

How did we get here?

In *Reality TV: Remaking Television Culture*, media scholar Mark Andrejevic writes of the 2000s: "Contemporary image culture teaches both the inevitability of contrivance and, paradoxically, the need to penetrate it—not just out of casual curiosity but in order to avoid the risk of being seen to be a dupe."

He writes that amid the constant monitoring of public spaces and life after 9/11 and a general distrust of Washington and its since-disproven "truths" about weapons of mass destruction leading up to the 2003 invasion of Iraq, a "savvy skepticism with naive empiricism" spread. This contradictory belief that one could see through a widely believed lie while also falling for another untruth led to the spread of conspiracy theories and myths like the idea that the Earth is flat or that aliens built the pyramids. It's a sort of paranoia gone wild, trained to shadowbox hidden forces and invent them should there not be enough at hand.

In this world, there's something reassuring about a villain. Better the devil you know than the devil you don't, and after the 2007 mortgage crisis, there were plenty of new seemingly invisible demons reshaping how millions of Americans lived, evicting families, accepting bailouts, quietly destroying American homes.

A villain isn't talking about hope and progress while selling out the country to private equity billionaires who will nickel and dime it, buying up the sense of reality that so many clamor for. A villain is not posturing as a good person while greenlighting genocidal slaughter. In America after the lies of the second invasion of Iraq and the mortgage crisis, when the invisible forces controlling lives turned out not to be as benevolent as they claimed, sometimes it seemed that villains had more integrity than the heroes.

A villain is just Heidi Montag wanting to make money for being famous. She just wants to follow her own path. Her "flaws" are on the outside, and she'll enumerate the ways in which she's tried to fix them, not squirrel them away so they can do damage in the dark. Villains may not be perfect, but at least you know who they are.

Reality TV, despite all the moral hand-wringing and critical disdain surrounding it, has never really been so different from other kinds of American media. It fits neatly into the broader cultural landscape of torn social ties, disconnection and alienation, and the hunger for a life that feels more real and the belief that video somehow offers a cure.

The genre may actually be most similar to the televisual medium that sits on the opposite end of the respectability spectrum, vaunted as so critical to maintaining the American republic: the news.

Around 1980, channels such as C-SPAN and CNN pioneered the idea that videos could mediate the reality of a universe that is too large and complex to be wholly perceived for people with limited time, attention, and sensory abilities. They promised to make sense of the world, packaging reality into digestible forms. The basic production teams used to tape news segments in the field are the same as the ones used to create reality TV. They can consist of field producers, camera operators, sound mixers, and assistants, collectively known as ENG (electronic news-gathering) crews. ENG crews append human organs—a microphone extends an ear, a camera puts an eye where it could not otherwise be—and the simulation of sensory input is just tantalizingly close enough to the real thing to keep viewers coming back in hopes of getting more.

News outlets claim to deliver reality undistorted, but that's not true. News media break reality down and repackage it into intelligible narratives. Viewers consume news that elicits strong feelings that people will keep coming back for. ENG groups record and package reality in similar ways whether they're working for MSNBC or Bravo, but one is seen as protecting democracy and the other, destroying it.

Plenty have crowed about Donald Trump using reality TV techniques to get attention in the news as though he were denigrating a sacred sphere. But Trump's success may come from realizing that news media and reality TV often operate in the same ways, delivering melodramatic feelings of reality while reporting election results, creating emotional arcs for votes to boot roommates from the *Big Brother* house or send a president to the White House. Voters want to feel real. They're tired of a world run by hidden forces too complex too fully understand. Trump's informality, his rambling speeches filled with jokes and bad dancing, make him seem more real than rival politicians who make eloquent promises to serve the country, then hand it to the spectral wraiths of private equity. Make America Great Again has a catchier ring than Make America Feel Real Again, but the same sentiment underlies both.

It was the way that Heidi marched into this contested terrain of reality in video that struck such a nerve. She was aware of the power of video to make life on-screen seem more than real, a kind of reality-plus or hyperreality, more authoritative than someone's unreliable lived experience. It's a strange psychosis that extends even to the military, where people are now hungry for "predator porn," or drone video proof of battlefield conditions, even when more than enough reliable information is available. Video is reality; someone's story of what happened isn't. Heidi was creating a new self, real enough for all to see.

But Heidi's transformation also shows that despite reality TV's supposed trashy radicality, it also appeals to oppressive norms and misogynistic ideas of what women should look like: big-breasted and blond. Reality TV isn't just a product of technological innovation used for conservative purposes; it's a product of reactionary American politics.

For years, using nonunion labor both in front of and behind the camera was one of the hallmarks of reality TV. Unions such as the Screen Actors Guild and the Writers Guild of America (WGA) had been organizing people working on scripted sets for decades, and reality TV offered network executives a workaround.

Media studies professor Misha Kavka has written about how federal deregulation in the 1980s made it easier for new channels to launch even though the overall audience size stayed the same. Advertisers had to spread their money around more at the same time that competition for talent increased. Over the decade, the average cost of a prime-time hour-long drama went up to more than $1 million, and producers were sometimes losing hundreds of thousands of dollars per episode. *Cops* was greenlit during a writer's strike in '88, and cheap-to-create clip shows such as *America's Most Wanted* and *America's Funniest Home Videos* showed how new kinds of programming could keep money flowing. Shows like this took off during this period.

Over the years, some workers on unscripted sets have successfully joined unions. They are still a small minority, but activists are trying to grow their numbers. Jed Holtz, an organizer for the Freedom Socialist Party and an art director on Food Network's *The Kitchen*, is working with the WGA to organize people working in what he calls nonfiction TV. The nonfiction label, as opposed to unscripted or reality, acknowledges that aspects of the shows may be scripted. Words such as a host's introduction or the presentation of challenge rules are often written by people—ostensibly writers—who could logically be represented by a writers guild but aren't because they're usually also doing a variety of other production tasks. But Holtz is working with the WGA to organize all the workers involved in a production into single union instead of having different trades organize themselves separately. "It's expanding the definition of storytelling in some ways," Holtz says, but he also asks the question, "How do we as workers . . . gain what we deserve for our labor, regardless of what that looks like?"

If the line between writers and nonwriters is blurring, then so is the definition of storytelling. Videos are not just flat windows onto the real world; everything about them is constructed. Camera angles, lighting decisions, set design, background scoring, editing, and performances all tell the story even if there are no writers, per se.

Heidi is a storyteller. She conceives her lines and delivers them in the moment, reacting to the scripts of the people around her, such as the newscaster interviewing her.

Many have followed in Heidi's steps—Christine Quinn, Donald Trump, the Kardashians—and they've been so successful because America had been heading in Heidi's direction since its founding. She is the self-made soul, speaking the story of herself into existence, redefining the wilderness as she sees fit, finding love and a home in the process.

This is the strange trajectory that hybrid homes get pushed along by the digital forces running through them. Video's paranoia about the story of reality now runs through the places we live.

The Real World, *Selling Sunset*, the Kardashians shows, and *The Bachelor* show how homes are freighted with feelings, but they don't explain why homes are just so foundational to the American psyche. Our homes, our selves. It might be a universal association, but Americans and their twisted economic system take it a step further. When it comes to your home, you have to own it, as any Real Housewife will tell you. It's on their show that we start to see how deep the paranoia about reality runs.

Who's going to take it from me?

Every American has been sold the idea that their home will satisfy multiple yearnings—to win, to feel safe, to have a family—but nonetheless American homes often leave people feeling like they're missing something, something that a different home, maybe a more expensive home, could provide. So many good feelings have become privatized and sold back to people that even just feeling whole has become a luxury. The alternative is to rely on digital deception to make life feel different than it is.

When the stakes are this high, it's not enough just to live in a home; you have to own it. Your home and the feeling of wholeness that it provides must be inalienably yours, lest someone or something try to take it away.

Homeownership is a norm of American culture. Americans have a silent faith in it that doesn't often need to be explained, but reality TV dramatizes the quiet yearnings of homebuyers, turning them into spectacles that put it all out there.

Searchlights shine into the night sky. A dancer waves feather fans from a balcony, and a man wearing a blazer over a bare chest opens the door so masked partygoers can enter a lofty atrium, where a woman in a white leotard hangs from a spinning ball. Cold light reflects off silvery fleurs-de-lis on the walls. Vaguely French furniture in shades of gray sits scattered across expansive, glossy white floors.

"This house is drop-dead gorgeous," says Porsha Williams, who arrives on the arm of her soon-to-be-ex. "This is a woman's castle."

Centuries of policies and philosophies have led to this pseudo-French mansion north of Atlanta. The promise of homeownership, the power of private property to define reality, the colonial worldview that underlies it all—there is no more complete embodiment of the forces shaping the way people live in the United States than this home, whose name is spelled out in light on its walls tonight: Chateau Shereé.

This is *The Real Housewives of Atlanta* and the home of its paradigmatic star, Shereé Whitfield, who has managed to grow along with the show through its sometimes chaotic evolution.

For years when I watched the *Housewives* shows, I thought it was weird how much they brought up homeownership. On every one of the franchises, it seemed like the women couldn't go a season without someone accusing someone of renting their home, like that was a crime. Who cares? It didn't seem to be a concern on any other show.

But the *Housewives* shows are not quite like the other juggernauts of reality TV. In some ways, the closest parallels are the programs of the franchise surrounding the Kardashian-Jenners, who are the recurring stars of their shows; but the Housewives are frenemies and not families. And unlike the Kardashians, the Housewives aren't in control of their shows. They get bopped about by the whims of producers, who hire and fire the stars at will. So the Housewives have some of the defensive energy of their modern farmhouse counterparts, but they don't have nearly as much power—gig workers rather than CEOs. Even with their over-the-top parties and delightfully tacky homes, they have more in common with the average American. Untethered, they get buffeted about in the breeze, making the Housewives better bellwethers of the unpredictable changes of modern life in the United States and the existential anxieties that get channeled into the places that average Americans live, albeit, most Americans don't live in anything quite like Chateau Shereé.

The Real Housewives of Atlanta has been about homes since its first minutes. The premiere opens with DeShawn Snow in her new

15,000-square-foot home in the Manor Golf and County Club, a private neighborhood in a wealthy suburb. She talks about having a staff of about half a dozen people, and she meets with candidates for estate manager. We meet the other cast members in their homes; NeNe Leakes lives in "an exclusive gated community," and Whitfield lives in a sort of Italianate mansion with stenciled walls, vaulted ceilings, and what appears to be a grand piano—not yet in her chateau.

The next episode splices a clip of Whitfield talking about her anticipated seven-figure divorce settlement with footage of her trying on new shoes in her living room. We learn that she loves fashion, and she spends the season "launching" her clothing line, SHE by Shereé, but she's unable to manifest it at what's meant to be her debut showing. ("A fashion show with no fashions—how dreadful.")

By the second season, Whitfield's old house is apparently in foreclosure because her ex-husband hasn't been paying the mortgage, so she's now in a less decadent home. SHE by Shereé remains in the works but still doesn't materialize. Whitfield sets to work on building a new "chateau" for herself, but the home remains nothing more than a weedy hole in the ground for some time. For years, the empty lot embodies Whitfield's inability to get anything done.

Delusional women have always been a big part of the *Housewives* shows; the franchise started by making them the butt of almost every joke.

The first series, *The Real Housewives of Orange County*, kicked off in 2006 with one foot firmly in the raunch era. Its first season included a cast member attending a party at the Playboy Mansion and a discussion of whether or not the women are MILFs. The show's premise was that it was a peek inside Coto de Caza, a gated community in Orange County, California, where, as it turned out, the good life wasn't all it was cracked up to be. The first few seasons featured wealthy, mostly white families in various states of disarray—divorce, juvenile detention, addiction—while living in multimillion-dollar mansions. There's some unintended irony when cast member Vicki Gunvalson says, "You know, people talk about, like, I want to be like the Joneses, like the neighbor next door that has all this—I think I am the Joneses. I think people want to be like us."

In *Cue the Sun!*, TV critic Emily Nussbaum writes that after the mortgage crisis, the Housewives and their decadent lifestyles became the object of class ire. They could have been the object of political ire, too, for liberals enduring the end of the second George W. Bush term: On the reunion after the second season of *Orange County*, all the women seem to say they are Republicans.

"A year ago I was getting ready, dressed in lingerie, to attend a Playboy Mansion party," Housewife Lauri Peterson says on the second season, when she is dating a wealthy new boyfriend. "Now I'm getting ready to attend a Republican party."

But the Atlanta Housewives offered something different when the show began—they were almost all Black, and none of them came out as Republicans—and they helped carry the franchise into the new era that swept the nation. The first season of the show ran in late 2008, and in the ensuing Obama years, liberals began to embrace suburban wealth and, as electoral maps evolved, vice versa.

The ire dissipated, and audiences started to laugh with the Housewives and not at them. Professional actors joined the casts, and the shows left behind their on-the-fly documentary style and became something like improv dramedies, with longstanding rivalries driven by years of repartee.

This shift consummated developments in the shows' home network, Bravo. In *The Housewives*, TV writer Brian Moylan recounts how in the early 2000s, executive Lauren Zalaznick transformed Bravo "from a channel into a brand," as he puts it, pivoting from sleepy arts content to reality shows with a wink and a sheen. *Queer*

Eye for the Straight Guy led the way, and a slew of slick de-alienated labor competitions, including *Project Runway* and *Top Chef*, followed. It was a world where talented strivers win and the lazy lose. By 2008, the channel had the highest educated and earning audience on TV, Moylan reports.

Frances Berwick, former president of Bravo, called this audience "affluencers," and where their tastes led, presumably, others would follow. Berwick took over as Bravo's executive vice president for programming and production in 2005, and under her, it pivoted away from competition and makeover shows and toward docusoaps such as the *Housewives* that focused on what Moylan calls "a camp performance of American affluence." These shows tapped into a more cynical and accurate view of reality in which wealth was not a reward for hard work but a sort of tacky accident. So what if your boss is a moron and makes triple your salary, these shows seem to say; life in their mansion is ridiculous, anyway.

The new, more respectable era of *The Real Housewives* ties together the workaholic and the camp by showcasing eccentric wannabes striving for success. No venture is too improbable or bizarre. In the third season of *Atlanta*, Phaedra Parks says she is buying a funeral home and Kandi Burruss plans to start a sex toy line. Parks explains the pair's passions in the next season: "Her imagination leads her into the world of sex, mine leads me into the world of the dead."

These women were strivers, modern Jay Gatsbys, only they weren't just social climbers, nor were they trying to get rich to win mates. They were chasing wealth and influence of their own—affluencers like their audience.

Whitfield, with her fumbled fashion line, doesn't always fit into this new mood, and after four seasons, she goes on hiatus, only to come back to the show a winner another few seasons later. Chateau

Shereé is finally no longer a dream but a 10,000-square-foot, five-bedroom, seven-and-a-half-bathroom home well on its way to completion. "Chateau Shereé is turning out to be the legacy I always wanted it to be," she says. "Not only for me but for my entire family."

But, relatably, even in her triumph, Whitfield cannot have peace.

While Whitfield was off the show, a new star took her spot and joined her in her building endeavors. Kenya Moore, an actor and former Miss USA, is building her manor just down the street from the Chateau. Moore found "a foreclosure, a really good deal," she says, and she's renovating a 6,500-square-foot home on a one-acre lot. "It is, architecturally speaking, a modern home, and I want to keep true to that form," she says about the structure stripped to its studs.

Whitfield and Moore are rivals—Moore was arguably Whitfield's replacement, and they occupy similar roles in their cast as sometimes-flamboyant drama queens. They trade barbs, cutting into each other's homes and digging into their stylistic differences in a discussion about detailing:

Moore: I don't do trim.

Whitfield: You need to do trim.

Moore: No, I don't need to do trim.

Whitfield: It's obvious. It's obvious.

Moore: No bitch is going to tell me I need to put molding and trim around my house.

Whitfield: Well, you need to do something if you want it to look good.

Later in that exchange, Moore—who in an earlier season famously twirled away from an argument while declaring herself, with a wink at the show's Southern setting, "*Gone with the Wind* fabulous"—attempts to walk away, but Whitfield calls after her:

"You wanna be all this and all that. You're shopping at IKEA and your shit ain't finished. Bitch, get out of here . . . Bitch, you why running away with your unfinished-ass house? . . . Bitch, twirl on some motherfucking baseboards."

In other scenes, Moore parodies the Chateau Shereé moniker to cast doubts on Whitfield's state and behavior: "Chateau She-can't-pay," "Chateau She-ain't-doing-shit," "Chateau She-ain't-done-yet," "Chateau Charade." Whitfield is a little more roundabout in her comments about Moore Manor, which sits in a sort of wooded dell, or, as Whitfield deadpans to the camera, "in the gully where the ogres live. Did she ask Shrek about me?"

Whitfield and Moore's exchange brings into focus more than their architectural differences.

Whitfield is a cast member from the original ridiculous era who was living off money from a divorce settlement and was unable to get her own business projects going. Moore was a new addition to the ensemble and apparently has her own money from an acting career. For all her over-the-top behavior, twirling away from conversations, she had a sort of gravitas in this wealth-obsessed world, and the former actor knew how to perform the role of the accomplished striver without the air of an arriviste.

The two characters' differing domestic styles imply a conflict of values. Moore was self-made and modern: IKEA and no trim, all this and all that. Whitfield was old-fashioned, a touch of one of Chekhov's three sisters dreaming of her new life in a chateau bedecked with molding and baseboards but seemingly unable to fulfill her fantasies and troubled by the rise of a savvy newcomer. She had hints of *Gone with the Wind* tragedy, the foil to Moore's fabulosity, clinging to the idea of her Tara to maintain a threatened sense of self.

Moore, on that glittering opening night at the chateau, continues to suspect that Whitfield is a fraud and is delighted when she peeks into Whitfield's basement and discovers that it is not done. Whitfield is furious, as though Moore has undermined her entire identity.

Whitfield's rival was a paragon of the winners of the Obama post–mortgage crisis era. In an earlier season, Moore had been evicted in a rent dispute and for a time lived in a hotel (with a white refrigerator, to the horror of castmate NeNe Leakes). Now she has found a foreclosure and renovated it in her own image. Whitfield, however, and her metonymic home still give off a whiff of crisis.

Whitfield says that after her divorce when she had to leave her home, "the kids and I went from castle to condo," and although she goes on to say, "Once the chateau is finished, I will be able to give me and my kids everything that was taken from us without the help of any man," the chateau may be owned by another woman—at least that's what Moore insinuates.

"Guess what," Moore says to Whitfield, "my name is on my house. It's not in my mother's name."

"Neither is mine, honey," Whitfield says, but later she tells other castmates that her house is in a trust and doesn't elaborate. Not owning her home was apparently something too horrible to speak much about.

Some of the shows' deepest beefs start with the suggestion that one Housewife rents her home or is still paying it off. A "new beginnings" party at the start of the fifth season of the Miami series devolves into a shouting match between erstwhile friends Lisa Hochstein and Larsa Pippen when the latter accuses the former of having a mortgage. Gizelle Bryant beleaguers Karen Huger on the Potomac franchise with accusations of renting big, only partially furnished homes in desirable locations for the show. In the second season of *Atlanta*, there's conflict between NeNe Leakes, Whitfield, and Kim Zolciak after Whitfield supposedly tells Zolciak that

Leakes rents her house. At the season four reunion, Leakes reverses the accusation, saying that Zolciak's new dream home is rented. "When you move into your dream home, you buy it, you don't rent it," Leakes says. The next season, Zolciak says that the new home of another cast member, the singer and songwriter Kandi Burruss, isn't in a great neighborhood. "At least everybody in my neighborhood owns their homes," Burruss retorts.

It's as though the mortgage crisis is a Freudian trauma at the root of the shows' dramas, foreclosure the unspoken threat looming just offscreen. In a sense, the *Housewives* shows are really about precarity in the post-crisis world. These women can be fired from the show at any moment for any reason. For many of them, the show is their main job. Their homes give them some semblance of solidity.

The Real Housewives franchise began late enough in the modern reality TV movement that audiences were skeptical from the beginning about how real the show was. It didn't help that the *Housewives* setup was contrived from the beginning. Anyone who thought very hard about it could see that the Housewives ensembles were clearly orchestrated; castmates were hired to create and maintain relationships with each other. And just as easily as a Housewife could be thrown into the cast, they could be thrown out. Accusing a castmate of being fake and phony was more than just a moral criticism of their sincerity—it called into question their suitability for their job.

If a Housewife doesn't own her home, does she really live where she says she does? Is she just pretending to be in Atlanta for the show while actually living in LA? Or is her whole lifestyle fake, and there's nothing real about her?

"I can do whatever I want in my house, and I don't have to worry about somebody taking it from me," Moore says. Whitfield responds, "Who's going to take it from me?"

The women's investment in their homes is much more than financial; it's emotional, even existential. Failing to own their homes endangers their job security, and their homes are linked to their basic safety. Both Whitfield's and Moore's homes are intertwined with their experiences with domestic violence. In Moore's case, the home itself is the object of her ex-lover's menacing—he smashed her windows and lurked outside. In Whitfield's case, the home is more symbolic. In one scene, she sits down with her allegedly abusive ex-husband, Bob, a former NFL player. She tells him: "Building the Chateau—it's something I have to do for myself and for my kids because I don't ever want to depend on a man because the man I was supposed to be able to trust—you left."

Their lovers are not the only menaces. There's also Andy Cohen. He's the puckish longtime producer of the shows who hosts the reunions at the ends of the seasons, when the women come together in a sort of roundtable discussion meets death match. Continuing the original concept of the show—that the good life is not as good as it seems—he kicks off multiple reunions by highlighting the artificiality of the Housewives' expensively done-up bodies, hair, and faces. He begins the third season's reunion by saying, "You ladies have no shortage of self-esteem, but it's not that easy keeping all your business up. I want to take a look at your assets." A clip package of their bodies follows, focusing on their breasts, butts, and cosmetic procedures. At the season 10 reunion Cohen proclaims: "Over the last decade, your hair, bodies, and faces have changed almost as much as your fashions," and a clip package follows showing their evolving looks. COVID offers no respite; the season 13 reunion starts with Cohen introducing a segment about how much the women ate while at home during the pandemic. He is reinforcing the doubt that the women are as they appear to be, eroding their ability to present themselves as they like, even at the most intimate level. He's cutting them down to size, similar to Juju Chang digging into Heidi Montag. A house, owned and enduring, offers some defense.

When Whitfield finally finishes the Chateau, she beams. "I feel like goddamn superwoman," she says. "I can do anything."

Whitfield's and Moore's homes represent their residents' whole selves and are proof of their reality. And though the Housewives may be a little more extreme than average in their psychological investment in their homes, they're not so different from many Americans.

"A man is not a whole and complete man," Walt Whitman wrote in 1856, "unless he *owns* a house and the ground it stands on."

Homes in the United States aren't important just because they mark status or offer retreats from cities or homesteads where people can supposedly isolate themselves from the world. They offer something more fundamental to people's identities—that is, if they are privately owned. Private homeownership is essential to the country's identity. And that's by design, although the situation could have been different.

Federal US public housing began in Atlanta. That's also where it ended.

"The city with the first public housing developments was the first to demolish virtually all of them," writes Akira Drake Rodriguez in *Diverging Space for Deviants: The Politics of Atlanta's Public Housing.*

Rodriguez lays out how public housing flopped in the United States after it gave the "wrong" people too much power.

Public housing started in the United States during the Great Depression with a paternalist patrician attitude to buoy down-on-their-luck people, primarily white people, during that exceptional time. Leaders envisioned public housing as a temporary way to help future homeowners get back on their feet, not as a permanent solution. Private homeownership, believed by capitalist leaders to be an inoculation against communism, was the goal. The program began in Atlanta.

Techwood Homes, which was only for white people, was dedicated in the city in 1935. University Homes, for Black people, opened there two years later. The federal Wagner-Steagall Act authorized local housing authorities the same year, and they began popping up across the country, but public housing really took off in the United States during the housing shortage after World War II, also the era of exploding suburbanization and the continued Great Migration. In Atlanta, leaders used public housing to enforce and deepen racial segregation while the Black proportion of the city's population grew, and the city annexed adjoining Black neighborhoods where planners essentially relocated Black people. The goal was segregation, but Rodriguez writes that postwar public housing projects in Atlanta also created environments where Black communities, particularly Black women, could organize. Federal resources supported public housing tenant associations, which Black women often led.

From the late '50s through the early '70s, the politics of public housing tenant groups evolved with this leadership. Housing projects became less of a temporary stop-gap for professionals facing tough times and more of a permanent solution for families who might never be able to leave the system. People became more vocal about what wasn't working in the buildings, protesting and organizing rent strikes. The tenants were getting in the way of business as usual for the city, which had long held a reputation as an exceptional space in the South.

"Atlanta has this motto of 'the city too busy to hate,'" Rodriguez tells me. "And it doesn't have those very sort of public desegregation battles . . . Most of those images are not coming out of Atlanta . . . and this is because they really wanted to position themselves as this modern city of the new South, where we have Black people that we talk to and we work with them, and these are our Black leaders who run our Black churches, and we have Black business owners who are millionaires."

By the mid-'70s, financial support for public housing and tenant associations started to dry up. The national economy hit some bumps, and Nixon pulled the plug on new projects.

A different approach to public housing assistance arose in the Reaganite '80s, a time of "compassionate conservatism" and privatization. Federal authorities developed the Section 8 program as an alternative housing method; it gave recipients vouchers that they could use to pay for rent in select private developments. Backers touted the system, saying it would give people more choices, a positive rhetorical veneer that papered over conservatives' complaints about "welfare queens" taking advantage of public handouts. The front of optimism flowered in a series of federal housing reform programs called Homeownership and Opportunity for People Everywhere—HOPE.

The first few HOPE programs offered limited housing assistance in various forms and more or less ended in the 1990s, but HOPE VI was the last and most consequential of the series. Rodriguez writes that it was meant to disperse concentrations of poor Black people. It provided grants for public housing agencies to demolish old buildings and redevelop them, often as mixed-income, lower-density, private developments. Atlanta was one of the first cities to employ the HOPE VI program; the first grant was for demolishing Techwood for athlete housing for the 1996 Olympics.

Original residents often didn't make the move to the new housing—they couldn't necessarily wait for the replacement homes to be built and moved on to other options. Myriad other new government affordable housing approaches addressed the issue piecemeal, and people scattered.

Tenant organizations withered. Dispersal makes it more difficult to organize. There's no single landlord or system to rally against, no close physical community. Even if the problems for scattered tenants are the same, it's not as easy to do something about them.

What power there was in public housing was lost.

"Without political representation or participation, Black people and spaces were demonized and cast aside as political and social deviants," Rodriguez writes. "Local and national uplift politics responded directly to these characterizations by focusing on assimilating Black behavior, political interests, and urban forms around white, middle-class, patriarchal, heteronormative capitalist norms."

HOPE, in other words, was a ruse. It and other new housing programs saw private ownership as the solution to public problems, but they did not solve underlying issues of the housing market and poverty—they just made it easier for developers to profit off of them. It was a win for the rich, white or Black.

By the 2000s, the city too busy to hate had become "a mecca for wealthy African Americans," as Leakes says in the first words spoken on *The Real Housewives of Atlanta*.

What happened to public housing in Atlanta reflects what happened across the United States. After decades of neglect and underfunding, even well-built housing projects have fallen into disrepair, and buildings that have reached the ends of their lifespans haven't been replaced. Any proposals introduced in Congress to revitalize the public housing system die on the vine. Meanwhile the US government subsidizes private homeowners with billions in tax deductions annually.

Homeowners, many businesspeople have theorized, are easier to control. Homeowners are too worried about making mortgage payments to go on strike. Homeowners can't pick up suddenly and move to look for better jobs. Homeowners aren't going to rally together against a landlord or whoever else because they're too focused on themselves.

As for the people too poor to ever become homeowners, they have to be confused to keep them on the defensive. Public housing had been managed by local administrations that created a relatively straightforward system to navigate. Now, poor people are served an abundance of "choice" programs that keep them occupied with the bureaucracy required to stay in them.

This dazzle-and-confuse strategy fits a larger pattern. The US government has a habit of ensconcing systems designed to protect private property at the expense of public interest in layers of obfuscation and bureaucratic mystery. These shrouds allow the government to veil destructive programs in beatific cloaks of hope and beneficence, to destroy communities while "helping" them.

In 1881, three years before *Ramona* came out, Helen Hunt Jackson published another book, this one nonfiction, titled *A Century of Dishonor.* Throughout hundreds of pages, Jackson detailed various ways the American government lied to and betrayed Native American communities in order to take their land, with accounts of civilian Anglo atrocities against Native people. The book wasn't the hit that Ramona was, but it did help spur the passage of a law that transformed land ownership in the United States.

For most of her life, Jackson wasn't involved in Native American politics. She was a poet and travel and lifestyle writer publishing in some of the biggest outlets of the time. She lived her later years in Colorado, but in 1879, she went to a Boston lecture by Chief Standing Bear of the Ponca Tribe and his interpreter Susette La Flesche, also known as Bright Eyes. They were raising money and attention to their people's campaign to move back to their homeland in what is now called Nebraska.

The Ponca Tribe had been screwed over by the United States in a way that would be unbelievable if it weren't so typical. The federal government made a treaty with the Ponca, recognizing their right to their land. However, in some mysterious bureaucratic blunder, the US later ceded that land to the Sioux Nation, so the Ponca Tribe was forced to move, leaving their homes and everything else. When some members of the Ponca Tribe left the new lands that they had been relegated to and tried to go home, they were arrested, and because Native Americans were not US citizens, they couldn't use US courts to try to get their rights wronged. They were stuck.

Standing Bear's account of the tribe's situation so moved Jackson that she joined a campaign among Anglos to return the tribe's land and set about writing her collection about the US government's mistreatment of Native American peoples.

"A full history of the wrongs they have suffered at the hands of the authorities, military and civil, and also of the citizens of this country, it would take years to write and volumes to hold," Jackson writes. "There is but one hope of righting this wrong. It lies in appeal to the heart and the conscience of the American people." She sent a copy of *A Century of Dishonor* to every member of Congress.

Her strategy worked, in a way, but Jackson did not live long enough to see the effects unfold. In 1885, just four years after *Dishonor* came out and one year after *Ramona*, she died a celebrated figure. Her friend Emily Dickinson wrote after her passing: "Helen of Troy will die, but Helen of Colorado, never." Historian Valerie Sherer Mathes has written about how others carried on Jackson's legacy—though not necessarily how she might've liked.

In Jackson's few years of activism she found allies in the Friends of the Indian group, which met at Lake Mohonk in upstate New York to figure out ways to "help" Native Americans by "civilizing" them and thereby empowering them in the US legal and social systems. This was the progressive solution to what was generally referred to by the Anglos as the "Indian problem," or the question of what to do with the people who inconveniently lived on the land that the growing United States was devouring. For much of the second half of the nineteenth century, the US strategy regarding Native Americans was to establish reservations for tribes, usually on relatively inhospitable land that Anglo settlers didn't yet want. The United States compelled tribes to become subsidiary nations to the US government, forbidding them from dealing with any other country directly. But the US government wasn't great at controlling its people, and Anglo settlers frequently intruded on Native American land no matter how remote, leading to violence and headaches for hapless bureaucrats and politicians loathe to restrain their constituents. Inevitably, Anglos eventually took back what land they had "given" to Native Americans when it came time to continue their relentless conquest of the continent.

Native American peoples often resisted Anglo expansion, frustrating US laypeople and government officials in their quest to exploit land and resources. The problem was deeper than just the toll of raids and counterattacks from the resistance; the "Indian problem" undermined the entire American project. As Jackson details, much if not all of the country was stolen from Native American tribes by Anglos who constantly lied and broke treaties to get the land on which the United States was built. The legal basis for the Anglos owning American land didn't rest on liberty and justice for all but deception, betrayal, murder, terror, and—in Jackson's words—dishonor.

Reformers such as the Friends of the Indian group thought they had a solution: privatize Native American land, give it to individual tribe members, and assimilate them into Anglo society. The colonized would become citizens and enjoy the full benefits of owning their land under the US system, supposedly preventing their land from being stolen again. This was the "kill the Indian, save the man" era, and even progressive Anglos at the time thought that Native American culture was worthless if not pernicious, so this kind of integration would give individual Native Americans their best shots at success. The idea was known as "allotment," and groups such as Friends of the

Indian advocated for it bullishly after Jackson's death. Eventually, they won. In 1887, Congress passed the General Allotment Act, also known as the Dawes Act for the Massachusetts senator who wrote it. Jackson's former allies saw it as the legacy of *Dishonor*.

The Dawes Act allowed the US government to allocate tribal lands to individuals within that tribe, but each person's allotment could only be so large—usually between twenty and 160 acres. Any left over or "surplus" land could be opened up to Anglo homesteaders. Many cash-poor people sold their land to Anglos. For Native American people overall, the act was a disaster.

Allotment ended in 1934, but it was too late. Native Americans held 138 million acres in 1887, but fifty years later, they had lost more than 90 million of those acres, reports Kristin T. Ruppel in *Unearthing Indian Land: Living with the Legacies of Allotment*.

Today, the legacy of allotment lives on in the nearly unnavigable ownership system it has left behind. One of the patterns of the United States' relations with Native American people is the government enacting half-baked "solutions" to Native American issues without consulting Native Americans or thinking through the full effects of Anglos' innovative ideas. The architects of allotment were no different.

Ownership of allotted land was not transferred directly to individuals. Because Anglos believed that Native Americans were incapable of responsible land ownership and had to prove that they could be good owners, land was initially placed in a trust by the US government. After a twenty-five-year probationary period, ownership was transferred if Native American people proved themselves worthy. In 1916, the federal government established a ceremony-slash-pageant to mark Native Americans becoming eligible to own land in which they would "shoot their last arrow," go into a teepee, and come out a changed person.

But if the government never deemed allottees worthy of the responsibilities of ownership, that land would stay in a trust to be inherited by the allottee's descendants. This trust land was then divided—or in legal jargon, fractionated—among the descendants, then continued to be fractionated by their descendants in perpetuity. There are legal restrictions placed on lands held in trust, so today, descendants of allottees own a fraction of their ancestors' land but cannot independently sell that fraction or develop that land. The Bureau of Indian Affairs manages the land for allottee descendants, often renting land out to Anglos, and Ruppel documents accusations of corruption against the department that claim it cheats Native American people out of their potential profits through sweetheart deals and poor management. Subsequent federal "solutions" did little to deal with such issues and often introduced new ones.

The more you learn about allotment, the more you probably want to scream. And that might not be accidental.

In *Dishonor*, Jackson focuses on the US government's roundabout way of pursuing its interests: "Early in our history was the ingenious plan evolved of first maddening the Indians into war, and then falling upon them with exterminating punishment"—a playbook any Housewife or genocidal state would recognize. Jackson documents a pattern of US citizens playing victim of Native American aggression by ignoring the many Anglo offenses that led to such hostilities. She writes of the Sioux: "The wonder is not that some of them were hostile and vindictive, but that any of them remained peaceable and friendly." She highlights the cold bureaucratic jargon that officials used to cover their aggressive intentions: "The phrase 'whether the Government shall determine to reduce the size of the reservation' sounds much better than 'whether the Government shall rob the Indians of a few millions of acres of land;' but the latter phrase is truth, and the other is the spirit of lying."

Genocide is not only an act of sprawling violence but a Kafka-esque process of the modern state executed in the style of the IRS and the Three Stooges.

HOPE and allotment not only show how a push for private homeownership can exploit people even while "helping" them but also reveal a belief in an almost metaphysical power of private property.

A 1887 Lake Mohonk conference noted that the Dawes Act offered "the Indians homes, the first condition of civilization." Jackson quotes an 1876 report from the secretary of the interior that says: "It is doubtful whether any high degree of civilization is possible without individual ownership of land." Communal stewardship of the land was not good enough. Only private property would bring what the whites wanted.

The United States is a nation of homeowners by design. Less than half the country owned their homes in 1920. At the time, homeownership was largely unaffordable—lenders often required 50 percent down payments and offered just five- or ten-year mortgages. But property ownership was not just a "civilizing" tool for colonizers; the prospect of it was central to the identity of white Americans.

Cultural historian Adrienne Brown has described how ideas about property ownership and personhood were linked as far back as the European Enlightenment and the beginnings of European colonialism. In English eyes, Indigenous people couldn't own the land; they just lived on it like animals did. The English considered property ownership a requirement for full citizenship; if other cultures didn't have the same conception of land ownership, then could their people be full citizens, even of their own countries?

Over the nineteenth and twentieth centuries, homeownership took the place of land ownership in the white American conception about the importance of property.

"There's nothing inherently moral about homeownership," Brown tells me, "and yet we are over about a century into a kind of manufactured ideology that homeownership is the most desirable way to live, the best way to live. It says something about your character."

Brown has written about how in 1931, President Herbert Hoover addressed the President's Conference on Home Building and Home Ownership, saying that Americans "never sing songs about a pile of rent receipts . . . to own one's own home is a physical expression of individualism, of enterprise, of independence, and of the freedom of spirit." Hoover talked about a "racial longing" for homeownership among white people. The establishment of the Federal Housing Administration in 1934 led the way for government-insured, longer-term mortgages, and by 1945 a majority of Americans owned their homes, mostly white people in all-white neighborhoods.

Private ownership decimated tribal power and traditional Native American relationships with the land. Ruppel writes: "The colonizer's dream of the assimilated native is the Christianized, detribalized, private landowner: the 'simulated white' of allotment."

The American dream of homeownership is a white colonial fantasy that endures not because it works out particularly well for most Americans but because alternatives have been systematically destroyed. The private housing market is also a useful tool to exploit people because it is so supposedly neutral and natural. It's a great way for white people to create a racist country without having to explicitly espouse racism.

"At some point in the early twentieth century," Brown writes in *The Residential is Racial: A Perceptual History of Mass Homeownership*, "white Americans stopped talking about residential discrimination in terms of personal feeling—as hatred, discomfort, or capacity—and started talking about it more consistently using the seemingly impersonal rubric of value—framing segregation as the protection of one's financial investment in property rather than as a matter of personal amity."

White people in the US have long used foreclosure and related legal tools to get Black people out of their homes. Starting in the Reconstruction Era, local governments used property taxes to drain Black homeowners of their new wealth and then seize the properties when owners were unable to keep up with the taxes. Assessors overvalued Black-owned lots, making it easier for their owners to fall behind on payments.

The practice continues in a similar form today. Cities and towns across the country regularly auction off unpaid property tax debt, which opens the door for the new owners of the debt to evict the homeowners, even if the debts are just a few hundred dollars. Activists and community groups are fighting such practices in cities such as Chicago, where tax debt sales disproportionately affect Black neighborhoods.

And back in the 1930s, when the federal government started insuring mortgages, it became an accepted truth that Black neighbors brought down property values. Wanting to live in all-white neighborhoods just made good financial sense—it wasn't personal.

Redlining, the government practice that mapped Black neighborhoods as unsuitable areas in which to provide mortgages in a banal bureaucratic process, reenvisioned the country, making racism a matter of the market, allowing it to thrive. It wasn't a dramatic, sensational thing that might excite the outrage of well-meaning white people, just a matter of maps and math.

As a result of being excluded from much of the housing market, Black people were more easily exploited, paying more for their homes and on worse terms, but Brown charts a continuing investment among Black Americans in the dream of homeownership that had roots going back to at least Emancipation. In the new era of increasingly abstracted racism, owning property still offered the dream of something concrete to build a good life on.

In the seventh season of *The Real Housewives of Atlanta*, Housewife Cynthia Bailey and her husband are opening a bar in the city. When she hears while touring a potential location that Martin Luther King Jr.'s body briefly rested next door, she lights up. "Martin Luther King—I mean, really, he had a dream. We got dreams," she says about her bar.

King's assassination spurred the passage of the 1968 Fair Housing Act, which banned redlining, but that has hardly solved the problem. Brown writes that the homeownership gap between Black and white Americans was larger in 2022 than it was in 1960.

Around the time of the mortgage crisis, when so many Americans, especially Black Americans, lost their homes, reality TV turned to a subtly seductive vision that offered a sense of superiority. The Atlanta Housewives, doing their part, sold a fantasy of life untouched by these concerns.

The last episode of the first season, which aired in 2008, is a reunion in which Andy Cohen reads a viewer email from "Kevin from San Diego": "I just lost my job. Most of my friends and family have hit hard times. Then I watch the show, and it looks the economy doesn't affect the Real Housewives. Do you ever feel guilty throwing your money away like that?" Cohen presses Whitfield to respond.

"Do I feel guilt about buying, you know, treating myself every now and then?" she asks. "No, I do not."

Cohen then pivots the segment to clips of a party in the bowling alley in the basement of the mansion of Lisa Hartwell, another castmate. "This is how we do it," Hartwell says.

—

In 1982, the cultural theorist Ien Ang published a book about the hit TV show *Dallas* in which she tried to explain the hold that the show had on audiences around the world. The primetime soap opera spellbound viewers with its storylines of romance and betrayal, including the third season's famous cliffhanger ending featuring the mysterious shooting of the show's main antagonist, J. R. Ewing. "Who shot J.R.?," became a pop culture headline, and the season four premiere was the most-watched episode of a TV show ever, surpassed only by the series finale of *M*A*S*H* three years later.

To understand the show's allure, Ang looked to the literary critic Peter Brooks's ideas about the popularity of melodramas and "the melodramatic imagination," which gives readers and audiences the feeling that the humdrum activities of daily life are more important, enriched with operatic intensity. Such a genre is a product of a modern age in which old providers of meaning like religion are receding and new worlds seem to erupt every day, defying attempts to understand them or order them into something greater than their parts. People turn to melodramas because they make mundane things, such as losing a lover, feel as important as national news.

"The melodramatic imagination should be regarded as a psychological strategy to overcome the material meaninglessness of everyday existence," Ang writes. It is "the expression of a refusal, or inability, to accept insignificant everyday life as banal and meaningless, and is born of a vague, inarticulate dissatisfaction with existence here and now."

Melodramas are nothing new. Brooks was writing about the nineteenth and early twentieth-century novels of Honoré de Balzac and Henry James, and melodramatic soap operas date back to the radio years, when stations would play them for women to listen to while they were isolated at home cooking and cleaning. For decades, soaps have been creating other worlds full of life and intrigue that audiences can tap into, and in doing so they have developed a technique of realism that allows the melodramatic imagination to thrive.

Soap operas have narrative continuity from one episode to the next, meaning that if a character discovers she's pregnant in one episode, she will be in the following one as well. The world of a soap opera does not reset at the end of an episode, as it does on a classic sitcom or a procedural crime drama. On *Law and Order*, for example, most episodes start with day one of a new storyline. The characters don't seem to remember much about the murders they were investigating the episode before. Soaps, however, use what is called a serial format in which storylines continue across episodes and seasons, developing arcs for years, even generations.

Seriality on TV is now commonplace outside of soaps—it's the norm for Outstanding Drama Series winners at the Emmys—but that wasn't always the case. In *Birth of the Binge*, media critic Dennis Broe describes how serial TV only started spreading from soaps in the Reagan years in shows such as the cop drama *Hill Street Blues*, which started on NBC in 1981. HBO later gave seriality an enduring sheen of prestige with its run of award-winning prime-time dramas that began in the '90s—the prison drama *Oz*, *The Sopranos*, *Six Feet Under*—shows that led a so-called golden age of television exemplified by serial dramas.

Seriality has roots in incrementally published nineteenth-century Western novels, such as those of Charles Dickens. Such novels, like the melodramas of Balzac and James, pursued a kind of literary realism that sought to more closely mimic lived experiences than earlier writing had, using specific but subtle innovations. In the essay "The Reality Effect," literary theorist Roland Barthes identifies a key technique of nineteenth-century literary realism that helped create the sense that the events of their stories were not just confabulations: Seemingly superfluous details such as the shape of a box heap stacked on top of a piano in a Gustave Flaubert novel, say, don't advance the plot or enrich the portrait of any character but create the feeling in readers that the events of the story are happening in "concrete" reality, or the real world. Such tidbits, Barthes says, make some novels feel real. He calls this the reality effect.

Seriality elicits a reality effect, too. The continuity creates the sense that stories exist in a larger world with time that progresses at a constant pace, independent of the bounds of a book or episode or dramatic five-act structure. The characters seem to be real people with their own lives that the stories just glimpse. But what happens when the characters in serial melodramas actually have real lives that continue off-screen? What happens to the melodramatic imagination when it's fed by reality?

The Surreal Life premiered in 2003. In the style of *The Real World*, the show took famous or formerly famous people and made them live together. Over its run, the show offered another chance at camera time for televangelist Tammy Faye Messner, rapper Flavor Flav, model Brigitte Nielsen, and many more. It was not a competition or a documentary or a noble-minded diversity experiment but a gonzo serial melodrama with a kaleidoscopic cast. The celebrity roommates partied, shared life stories, fought, and dated while sharing a house. Audiences knew that the castmates' lives continued off the show because many had been tabloid staples for years. There could be no illusion that the characters would disappear after the episodes ended. And viewers, who tuned in en masse, loved it.

The series spawned a galaxy of additional shows: Flav and Nielsen coupled up on the third season of *The Surreal Life* and got one of the series's many spin-offs, *Strange Love*, but they broke up, and Flav got a dating show, *Flavor of Love*, which led to a series for that show's first runner-up, *I Love New York*, the first of many shows for enduring icon Tiffany "New York" Pollard. The shows composed their own romantic subgenre: *Rock of Love with Bret Michaels*, a dating show with the lead singer from the 1980s glam rock band Poison, adapted the format and feel of *Flavor of Love* by having women line up to date a past-his-prime music star without being directly connected to the mothership show. Brian Graden, who oversaw programming at VH1 and acquired *The Surreal Life* for the channel, tells me, "At one point we had seventeen, I want to say, spin-offs. There was no television franchise that ever did that."

Audiences were captivated by how *The Surreal Life* and its offshoots twisted early-2000s reality TV and pop culture more generally into a parody of itself. Graden had already been successful in rejuvenating VH1 in the early 2000s with the *I Love the . . .* series of shows that explored the culture of earlier decades—*I Love the 70s*, *I Love the 80s*, and so on. Ironically, Graden says, the shows and their seemingly nostalgic themes attracted younger audiences to the channel who weren't watching to relive their glory days but for something else. But what?

The Surreal Life offers some clues. It was not about recreating fond memories—its audience was too young to have lived through the heyday of the stars on the show—and it wasn't some fictionalized fantasy. *The Surreal Life* and its descendants reimagined real life as a place where the past could be reinterpreted, even humiliated, for a younger audience's pleasure. Boldface names of yesteryear were forced to give up their privacy, bunk together in shared bedrooms with curtains for doors, do their own housekeeping, and have all their calls recorded like any run-of-the-mill *Big Brother* contestant entertaining Joe Couch Potato back home. These shows made viewers feel superior just for having the good sense to tune in.

"If you watch *Rock of Love*, it was not *The Bachelor*," Graden says. "It did not have the same earnestness. It was in on its own joke to some degree."

The audience's sense of superiority is ironic, given they are still in thrall to shows that aren't necessarily the most genius things ever created.

"It is perhaps part of our postmodern sophistication that we don't quite take melodrama 'straight' anymore," Brooks writes. But "however sophisticated we have become, the appeal of the melodramatic remains a central fact of our culture."

Audiences had always known that the reality simulated by nineteenth-century novels or twentieth-century soaps was not actually reality. People knew that the characters didn't go on living when they put down the book or turned off the TV. The reality effect brought with it a knowingness that just because something *felt* real didn't mean that it was. Viewers brought that skepticism to reality shows as soon as they began, questioning whether the Louds in *An American Family* were being honest about their lives and how much of the show was orchestrated if not scripted. *The Surreal Life* and its progeny leaned into that skepticism, rewarding their audiences' sense of savvy and superiority, even though those characters did go on living after people stopped watching. Reality effects such as seriality work differently here because the shows feel real but are also so wildly different from the day-to-day life of someone sitting at home in Idaho that the feeling of reality gets a little jumbled.

The *Surreal* shows are definitely reality TV, but they reflect a fractured reality, where the camera isn't just passively recording what is happening. On these shows, the lens and the audience behind it are reordering the hierarchies of the world, humbling stars into begging for attention. These shows offer a surreality effect—the feeling of reality, but a reality different from the "concrete" world that physically exists, an altered reality in which the audience feels itself to be more powerful than it is.

Melodrama "tells us that in the right mirror, with the right degree of convexity, our lives matter," Brooks writes. A surreal melodrama not only helps audiences believe that their lives matter but helps them believe that their realities are different than they are, selling a false sense of power that audiences in an increasingly unequal country lack.

This surreality effect has metastasized across reality TV and its spaces.

The *Housewives* shows have a subtle way of spreading surrealism and breaking out of the screen: the confessionals. These are the moments when one of the show's subjects sits in a room and talks to a producer, who is off-camera, about the events on the rest of the show. Confessionals have been a part of reality TV since *The Real World*, and they're part of a variety of shows that have even a partial documentary format—*Survivor*, *The Bachelor*, and *The Kardashians* all incorporate them. Usually one subject is featured at a time and the other subjects don't know what someone says in confessionals until they watch the show air. The confessionals take place in a special non-place relative to the world of the rest of the show; on fishbowl shows like *The Real World*, the confessional space is often a room in the house that is not shown using cameras other than the single still camera in the room. Although it is physically in the house in the "concrete" world, the confessional room does not exist in the narrative world of the show. It is an exceptional space that exists outside the rules of space and time. Scenes can cut back and forth from confessionals; subjects speak in confessionals as though the events they are discussing are happening in the present tense even though they aren't; and the confessional scenes are usually shot much later. The *Housewives* shows usually use green screens to make it seem as though the subjects are doing confessionals in their homes, typically, but they're actually in a studio. The backgrounds are often completely still with a soft focus, giving them a dreamy quality—an imagined double of the Housewives' homes where the rules of regular existence don't apply.

In the confessionals, the world of the rest of the show breaks. This used to be unlike scripted TV; *Dallas* never had moments where the characters suddenly existed out of the space and time of the rest of the show and confessed their feelings to the viewer. Scripted shows such as *The Office* and *Abbott Elementary* adopted confessionals to mimic reality TV, and now confessionals have become another common technique to create a sense of realism.

Confessionals are similar to moments when a character breaks the fourth wall and speaks directly to the camera, creating an effect that the person on-screen is looking at and talking to the viewer and the two are having an interaction. But direct-to-camera moments are not genuine interactions—there is no real back-and-forth, and the person on-screen will never hear the person in front of the screen. They are failed simulations of social interaction and reinforce the feeling of an uncrossable divide between the melodramatic universe behind the screen and the "real" world in front of it.

In reality TV confessionals, however, the person on-screen usually doesn't look directly at the camera and instead looks at a producer interviewing them just to the side of the camera. It's as though the audience is eavesdropping on an intimate conversation, and there's no disappointment of a failed simulation. There is instead an opening up of the universe of the show. Reality TV subjects exist not only in the space and time of the melodramatic plot but also in this other confessional world, with its own relationships and situations. They are able to travel across these universes and step into others, into aftershows, spin-offs, and fan conventions—all kinds of offshoots that the *Housewives* shows have spawned in multitudes. The unity of the melodramatic universe is fractured, and any number of narrative worlds are possible. There's no longer an impregnable surface in between the concrete reality of the viewer and the characters in the melodramatic space on-screen. There is instead a kind of scaffolding of worlds between the domain behind the camera and the one in front of it, supporting digital-physical hybrid homes as they extend around us.

Barthes's reality effect gives the feeling that fiction is happening in a real world. The surreality effect of unscripted serial melodramas such as *The Real Housewives* lets this feeling of reality flow into our real world, covering what actually exists with the feeling of an imagined reality, a kind of hyperreality. In this layered space, the melodramatic imagination runs amok, no longer bound by a discrete fiction, twisting anything it can find. On-screen homeownership in this context is powerful, able to turn one woman's manor into a balm for millions who get to enjoy the feeling of homeownership regardless of their own living situation.

Brown writes about how various institutional branches of American society insisted that "only white men were real men" in the 1920s, when the modern real estate market was born. During the Great Depression, losing your property was something akin to losing your whiteness. To be fully real in this market, you not only had to look white, but you had to *feel* white, and one of the main ways to do so was by owning a home. Over the past century, inscrutable financial and bureaucratic systems have decreased a feeling of reality, and those systems sell a physical feeling of reality back in the form of buildings, homes. Reality for sale.

Which is not to say that everybody buying a home just wants to feel white—but everyone buying a home may want to feel real.

"I'm so proud of myself for being self-made," Moore says while talking about her manor, built from the bones of a foreclosure. "Everything I do I built from the ground up." She dreams of rebirth: "This home will make me finally feel rooted," she says. "This is where my life will begin again."

The surreality of melodramas such as *The Real Housewives* lets viewers feel that feeling of rootedness and pride themselves as they cheer for the triumphant homeowners on screen, feel joy in watching a woman buy her home. Her win is our win, like that of a champion sports team. *The Surreal Life* brought celebrities low and made audiences feel superior, but in the celebratory *Housewives* melodramas, everyone ascends, viewers and homeowners alike, providing a feeling of triumph in a time when more and more people were losing.

Whitfield most embodies a personal investment in her home, but it's another of her castmates who embodies an emerging post–housing crisis relationship to ownership. In a world burned by the property market, savvy owners have developed a dispassionate approach. Kandi Burruss is a fan favorite with multiple spin-offs and the most Instagram followers of any Bravo star. And though Kenya Moore may have been Whitfield's nemesis, Burruss was Whitfield's foil.

Throughout the show, Burruss is the level-headed, sensible one while also potentially being the wealthiest, having had a Grammy-winning singing and songwriting career when she was younger. "I have fame and fortune, and I've earned it," she says in the title sequence for the third season. Despite her wealth, she starts out her time on the show in a relatively modest home that she bought when she was nineteen. She's hesitant to move into something grander, though she could, and eventually she does move into a seven-bedroom house with an indoor swimming pool.

All the while, Burruss maintains a humble image. In the tenth season, two castmates, Marlo Hampton and Porsha Williams, get into a spat. Hampton says Williams's doormat is too small; Williams cries. In the next season, in a callback to the fight, Burruss confesses with a laugh that she doesn't have any doormats at all.

"I'm one of those people that's kinda guilty of never finishing their house," Burruss says later, the implication being that she's always working, launching businesses, striving for more.

Unlike Moore and Whitfield, Burruss doesn't live in one of the traditionally luxe areas of Atlanta, such as Alpharetta or Buckhead, which Parks calls "the 90210 of the South." Burruss, with her

Grammy and platinum records, doesn't need to prove the status of her reality.

Burruss, whom cast members often speak of in reverential tones, is something of a hero in the celebratory capitalist era that the show entered around its thirteenth season in 2020. At that time, cultural shifts again pushed the *Housewives* shows in a new direction. Conversations about race and the portrayal of Black people on camera in the wake of George Floyd's murder likely played a role, but the blockbuster success in 2019 of *Selling Sunset* and its visualization of a new era of girlboss femininity may have been more important. In its wake, *The Real Housewives of Atlanta* did away with stock background music and adopted a pop and hip-hop soundtrack, added slow glamour shots of the women arriving at events, and embraced a more exultant tone overall. Casting shifted across the *Housewives* franchises, too—the Miami version cast a medical doctor, Potomac cast a professor, and Atlanta, in what was surely not a nod to the end of the city's public housing system, cast an Olympic gold-medalist, Sanya Richards-Ross. The shows had evolved from ridiculing the wealthy to celebrating their credentials.

Burruss blended easily with this shift. "I think everything you do should inspire you in a way that you can make more money," she says in season nine. By that point, on top of releasing new music, she had launched numerous businesses: her sex toy line, the web show *Kandi Koated Nights*, a musical that Burruss wrote and starred in, and a line of baby clothes and accessories named for her young son, Ace. She has since opened multiple restaurants, started the podcast *Kandi Koated Live*, toured her own burlesque show, and launched a makeup line in between other acting and production gigs.

Burruss doesn't have a metonymic home. The closest she has is the Kandi Factory, an office space that she bought for herself, but she seems to have detached herself from emotional investment in her home. Burruss presents a third option beyond homeowner and non-homeowner perfectly suited for the private equity age: investor. On the tenth season, in a scene in the Kandi Factory, Burruss tells her employee, DonJuan Clark, that she just put in an offer on the property across the street. Clark is exasperated. He thinks Burruss is overextending herself. Todd Tucker, Kandi's husband, backs Burruss up. "Who wins in Monopoly?" he asks. Burruss responds: "The people who own the most property!"

Brown points out to me that Burruss learned to profit from ownership at an early age. Although Burruss found fame in a pop group of her own, Xscape, she found fortune also by writing and cowriting—and owning or co-owning royalty rights to—songs such as the Grammy-nominated hit "No Scrubs" for '90s superstars TLC. Her authorship gave her ownership and brought her wealth.

Brown also points out a connection to home-flipping shows, such as HGTV's offerings, which have normalized a Burrussian sense that homes can be abstract financial assets and not physical spaces with deep cultural connections.

Flipping shows rarely, if ever, explore the backstory of why a house is in disrepair. The shows make it seem natural, as though the house had just aged and fallen into ruin. But often, the people who used to live in those homes were squeezed by racist systems. Maybe they were overtaxed or loan officers refused to extend them credit for maintenance that white homeowners would have gotten easily. The shows don't get into how, say, a historically Black neighborhood gets destroyed and repackaged as an affordable option for young white buyers looking to live somewhere cool or "up-and-coming." All that has disappeared from flipping shows, just as redlining made real estate racism invisible. But the narrative structure of flipping shows, with its transformative reveal of a redesigned home, makes all that structural racism also feel good.

This investor mentality that sees homes only as assets for people to buy and sell is celebrated by online influencers peddling lifestyles of financial optimization and advice about how to retire early by buying properties and turning them into Airbnbs. This version of the American Dream is about succeeding in a world of unfettered competition, even though only a select few can win and the rest of us are just watching.

The grinding efficiency of this system is why the world feels like it's becoming less real even though it's not. There's no metaphysical catastrophe unfolding around us. We are not all about to vanish. It's just that the things we have been told we need to be real are getting further out of reach. And now, as the possibility of ownership and the feeling of reality that comes along with it are taken away, hybrid homes trick us into feeling like we're better off than we are, haunted by lingering reminders that we're still mucking through the dirt.

On Bravo, the *Real Housewives* shows are now often eclipsed by a newer franchise with higher ratings: *Below Deck* and its many spin-offs, which follow the crews of luxury yachts while they serve rich guests. These shows present a fantasy of an ideal workplace with a strict hierarchy, overseen by a stern but benevolent boss in the form of the ship's captain. Crew members who underperform or break the rules are swiftly expelled from the vessel and the show. These are not the de-alienated competition programs of yesteryear, such as *Project Runway* and *Top Chef.* On the *Below Deck* shows, victory in competition just means keeping your job and collecting a nice tip.

"What the 'reality' in 'reality television' seems increasingly to signal is this aestheticization of occupational activity, in a perfect marriage of aesthetic conviction with capitalist competition," writes Sianne Ngai in *Our Aesthetic Categories.*

On *Below Deck*, the owners of the boats are never on-screen. They're not playing the same game as their subjects. The real winners of modern competition aren't competing at all; they're setting the rules from the sidelines, watching while the rest of us battle ourselves to bits.

In the surreal world, most of us are left to savor the victories of others as our own. Reality is now not a competition so much as a trap.

Open your eyes

Americans live in cruel homes. People think that owning a home will transform them, but cruel homes make people feel lacking—in security, company, stability, love—even while promising to provide those things, a cycle leading to people feeling hollowed out, scraped to the point of feeling separated from themselves, not feeling real even while being tricked into thinking they're better off than they are. Cruel homes sell back bits of the feeling of reality that they take away.

This cruelty isn't uniquely American. It has roots in some of the most fundamental ways that many people think about being in the world. It springs up through the origins of colonialism from the basic promises of Christianity that find a perfect vessel in which to blossom in America. And in hybrid homes, those vessels take some surprising shapes.

Consider *Trading Spaces*, TLC's classic home-improvement show, which I took in as a teenager, slack-jawed, on afternoons in the early 2000s. *Trading Spaces* was a happy show with its bright colors, funky background music, and radiant host, Paige Davis, with her perfect pixie cut. Mostly the show was comforting and fun, not cruel, and it inspired me to paint my bedroom a questionable hot dog combo of mustard yellow and ketchup red. Like millions of others, I was rapt by the show's positive glow.

Trading Spaces had a pretty simple structure: Every episode, neighbors swapped homes for a couple of days, and with the help of designers and carpenters and $1,000, redid one room in each other's homes. At the end, the neighbors would go back to their homes, and cameras would watch while they saw their new spaces for the first time. Some of the renovations were modest—new wall colors, rearranged furniture, and built-in shelving, maybe—and others were more extreme: a basement turned "beach" with real sand covering the floor, an upside-down room with the furniture hanging from the ceiling. Reactions varied from squeals of joy to sobs.

The show traveled around the United States, featuring different residents each time and a rotating cast of designers, who became the show's stars alongside Davis and the carpenters. It premiered in 2000, originally in a 4 P.M. weekday slot, but when it was so successful, executives added a prime-time airing. It became a smash and was nominated for prime-time Emmys in 2002 and 2003. It was light, it was fun, it was breezy. It was a hit.

Ty Pennington, who was one of the show's on-screen carpenters, became a particularly popular personality on the show, and he tells me about a Beatlemania-esque moment when fans mobbed one of the show's sets: "I couldn't even get to my car to get out, and I had to put a trash can over my head, and like, I could smell, like, the garbage juice that was already dripping on me. And I was like, wow, so this is it. This is fame. Like, it smells like garbage."

"It was a movement," Genevieve Gorder, another of the show's designers, tells me. "It wasn't just a show."

Trading Spaces changed TV by showing how popular a jazzed-up home-improvement show could be, and in its simple format lay the essence of an emotional structure that has shaped the world.

More immediately, though, *Trading Spaces,* which was a riff on an earlier British show called *Changing Rooms*, evolved out of an emerging branch of the reality TV tree that sprouted from PBS's *This Old House,* which Doug Wilson, another of *Trading Spaces*'s featured designers, calls "the original of the original of the original." He declares that "*This Old House* was the first reality-based show."

This Old House does arguably have a claim on the title, though again, it's hard to say definitively what was the first reality show. The show, which premiered in 1979 on WGBH, a Boston-area public channel, features a different home getting remodeled every season. Bob Vila was the original host of the show, and the gig made him a national star. He left it in 1989, but others took over, and as of when I'm writing this, the show is still running.

This Old House is an example of instructional TV, which is as old as TV itself. Early noncommercial stations aired instructional content showing viewers how to do things like prepare a home budget or arrange flowers, part of the government's mandate that TV should serve society, and early programs included cooking shows such as Julia Child's, launching her as one the era's biggest lifestyle TV celebrities. Her show, *The French Chef,* was produced by WGBH from 1963 through '73 and was a precursor to the what was to come: Russell Morash created *The French Chef* with Child and went on to create *This Old House.*

Instructional home TV found outlets on new cable channels launched in the 1970s and later.

TLC, which once stood for The Learning Channel, had its origins as another kind of educational platform in the '70s. It started as an initiative by Appalachian states to broadcast content that could be used in schools and universities. It became a commercial network in 1980 and eventually Discover, Inc., the company that owned and operated the Discovery Channel, took control of it in '91 and began moving it away from educational programs to reality shows for a general audience: medical shows such as *Trauma: Life in the E.R.* and some home-improvement shows in the style of *This Old House*.

Home and Garden Television, or HGTV, got a later start in 1994, and it was years before it turned into the behemoth it is today, but it quickly found an audience. It was the brainchild of Kenneth Lowe at Scripps, a national media company, who saw a rising interest in home design as the baby boomer generation came into its homeowner glory. This was the era when Martha Stewart found TV fame with her *Living* show, which sold the idea that housework could be fun, perfected, even glamorous. HGTV's content was more mundane, but it delivered on the promise of its name: hours of shows about homes and gardens, typically instructional content about DIY projects. An avuncular man might show how to install a bat house on a home and harvest the guano for fertilizer; a bespectacled woman might explain how to paint an animal print on an unfinished ceramic vase. Carol Duvall, a Midwestern white mom, ruled the roost with her popular crafting show. All in all, the channel's content was not as utilitarian as the stuff you might find on *This Old House*, more the kind of thing that could inspire a weekend project for a suburbanite looking to give their place some personality, and nothing that would capture the national imagination like its shows would decades later.

Throughout the '90s, home improvement was a pretty gentle genre. It may have gotten a morbid boost in 2001, the year after *Trading Spaces* debuted. "People after 9/11 were nesting," Wilson tells me. "They wanted to feel comfortable."

Similar to how COVID-19 lockdowns were boons for shelter magazines, September 11 could've inadvertently pushed people to the show, which focused not only on the comforts of home but also familiar neighbors. *Trading Spaces* relied on having friends next door whom you knew well enough to give them the keys to your home and let them sleep in your bed while they redecorated your space—potentially an appealing idea to a country swept with racist panics about supposed sleeper-cell terrorists lurking down the block.

Audiences didn't just want to watch the show; they wanted to be on it. "People wanted to be with us," Davis tells me. The show had plenty of suspense-building scenes of designs going awry, but it had just as many if not more clips of pure banter between the host, designers, carpenters, and residents.

Trading Spaces followed in the tradition of its instructional predecessors, but it emphasized entertainment more than education. Segments sometimes felt like regional theater improv comedy skits, with kooky designers butting heads with exasperated carpenters or chatting with homeowners about their favorite date-night meals. Producers actually wanted the show to be more instructional. "That was sort of the main note we would always get," Davis says. "The producers were often begging us to please give real information instead of just talking about, like, that we love spaghetti." The show was like a very little forerunner of the Kardashians, offering the experience of just hanging out with friends.

But *Trading Spaces* also had an extra emotional dimension to it that went beyond the fun company it provided to viewers. It tapped into something more profound than other reno shows, something best illustrated by the episode featuring a character who came to be known as Crying Pam.

Pam Herrick and her husband, John, lived in Puyallup, Washington, a small city in the Seattle–Tacoma area. They went on the show with their neighbors, Laureen and Charles Jobe, trading their homes with a reservation: They didn't want anyone to touch their fireplace. Doug Wilson, the designer of their space, however, did just that, covering their brick mantel in white wood as part of a neutral-tone design scheme. At the end of the episode, Davis leads the Herricks through the reveal ritual: They return to their space, and Davis escorts them with their eyes closed into the redecorated room so the cameras can record them seeing their new space for the first time.

"Open your eyes and see your new family room," Davis says.

The couple opens their eyes. John says, "Wow." Pam, her lips pulled tight and her hands in fists, opens her eyes. She looks around and smiles. "Well," she says and wheezes out a laugh. "I really like the wainscoting."

"You do?" Davis asks excitedly.

"I really do," Pam says.

"It's different," John says and blinks. Pam points out the new slipcovers approvingly. John shakes his head.

Then Davis asks them what they think about the fireplace.

"You guys are gonna be fixing that in a little bit," Pam says. John mumbles about firewood and looks around uncertainly. Pam grins and shifts her jaw before whispering to Davis: "I'm gonna have to leave the room now."

"You're that disappointed?" Davis asks, and Pam responds, "Well . . . I'm gonna have to leave the room," barely getting the words out before walking out of frame.

She audibly sobs off-camera while Davis asks John if they can fix anything. "I don't even know where to start," he says, and they talk a little more before eventually walking out of frame to console crying Pam.

"We were there to be provocative," Wilson tells me. "We were on-camera to promote something beyond everybody's normal, you know, existence."

Throughout his time on the show, Wilson was no stranger to eyebrow-raising ideas: He once turned a bedroom into a "prison of love," decorated in shades of gray, complete with a mural of an intake holding tank at the top of a wall. But Pam's room wasn't nearly as outrageous. It was pretty simple, actually. Wilson put some gray paint on the walls and traded chintzy seating for somber slipcovered chairs, plus the white wainscoting that Pam liked and the covering added to the fireplace, which Wilson tells me was designed to be easily removed. Were it not for the tears, the renovation would have been pretty unremarkable, but Pam couldn't see past the covered fireplace.

Pam's reaction became emblematic of the show.

"The cynical thing to acknowledge," Davis tells me, "is that it's what put us on the map."

Crying Pam was a star-maker, and the drama of emotionally unpredictable reveals helped propel *Trading Spaces* to a level of success beyond its peers.

But back in 2000 when the show began, breakdowns weren't the goal of the show; a gentler surprise on the part of homeowners was. Wilson says the original concept was for neighbors to ease each other out of whatever stylistic ruts they had fallen into.

Usually, contestants applied to be on the show in pairs of neighbors; instructions advised them to live close enough that the production crew could quickly walk between them. Before taping, producers asked residents to describe what they did or did not want done to their homes. Designers used this to plan out what they would do.

"When they come to your house, the design is set," Julie Tarr, a homeowner on season two, tells me.

Wilson says the designers would collect information about the homeowners, what they wanted, and what they wanted to do for their neighbors. Though most of the show's handful of designers played it safe, Wilson and another, Hildi Santo Tomás, did not. They became notorious for upsetting homeowners or creating impractical spaces—furniture on the ceiling, beach in the basement.

"Our show was a game show," Wilson tells me. He wasn't afraid to give contestants things they might not have wanted.

Press coverage labeled Wilson and Santo Tomás "villains" of the show, something Wilson does not embrace, but he doesn't say he was misrepresented. He says that the show's producers didn't goad him into creating controversy. They didn't need to amp him up—he was already amped up.

Wilson studied acting when he was young, and as he tells it, lessons from that experience inspired him and Hildi to take the reins:

"I was approaching it from more of a theatrical but livable standpoint," he says. "Hildi turned it into completely theatrical installation and hardly livable."

"This is why I love *Trading Spaces*," Santo Tomás says in Julie Tarr's episode while spray painting a couch. "I can just get an idea and do it!"

Wilson and Santo Tomás, who did not respond to my attempt to get in touch with her, may have been the most provocative, but all the designers seemed to base their schemes on the flimsiest concepts.

"Every time you do a room, you have an object that is the foundation of your inspiration," Davis says to Genevieve Gorder, the other designer on Tarr's episode, who has glommed on to an obi, a Japanese sash, that she brought with her to the homes. "Sometimes it's a piece of fruit," Davis says, "sometimes it's a flower, and this time it was that obi."

This kind of random inspiration is pretty common on the show. Generally, the show features suburban spec homes that lack any architectural individuality. The homes are just developer specials, the products of real estate formulas pasted over the terrain with little evident consideration of their environs, much less any considerations for the culture of their future residents. The owners are usually relatively young and middle class and generally don't have the money to buy distinctive furniture or art, so the designers create culture out of fruits and flowers, their tacked-up constructions the simulation of a culture's artifacts. And the shock of having to accept, alone and exhausted after two days of work, what the designers come up with is too much for some.

When Davis reveals Gorder's obi room to its owners, Nancy and Lennie Puetz, Nancy initially smiles and laughs before ambivalently remarking on the colors of the walls. Lennie stays more upbeat and says he likes the fabric on the pillows on the couch. "I'm . . . not sure," Nancy says, tears welling up in her eyes. Davis asks if she likes the idea of them. "Not really," Nancy says before wiping her eyes.

It was in such moments that the latent suffering of suburban American existence shaped by uncaring economic formulas and cold bureaucracy became acute, summoned by the ritual that marked the end of every episode and had its origins in the beginnings of reality TV: the reveal.

The show's emphasis on reveals goes back to that old reality progenitor, *Candid Camera*. At the end of the ruses on that show, the deceit would be revealed to the subject ("Smile, you're on *Candid Camera*!"), and emotions followed. The reveal revealed two things: the situation's deceit to its subject and the subject's reaction to the audience. Would they laugh it off or threaten the camera with a fist? Or would the audience lose, and there be almost no reaction at all?

Strong reactions of any kind are the goal.

Crying Pam's reveal was included in a *Trading Spaces* compilation released by TLC on DVD in 2003 titled *They Hated It!* Not simply *They Hated It*, which would be a straightforward report of suffering. There's the exclamation point—*They Hated It!*—indicating the audience's delight.

But everyone I talked to about the show was adamant that the whole process was usually genuinely enjoyable for the cast and contestants.

Though producers were eager for the contestants to express themselves, the people I talked to who appeared on the show said they never felt pressured to say or do anything dramatic. Apparently, no one was plied with alcohol or kept up late just to force them into a messy breakdown. The reveals weren't faked or shot twice. The renovations were really done in two days on $1,000 budgets by the designers, carpenters, and residents.

Gorder says, believably, that the show democratized design. When it started, affordable home decor store options were limited to places such as Home Depot, IKEA, or department stores, she says. Everything else was for the rich.

Gorder paints for me a bleak, if accurate, picture of middle-class American living at the time that I recognize from my years in Poughkeepsie: "Everyone had beige. They had the halogen lamp in the corner that, you know, shined up. It was black, you know the exact one . . . they had the oatmeal, thick plush wall-to-wall carpet, huge TV that was probably three feet thick. No window treatments, no paint, no molding. It was hollow . . .'Cause it was about builders doing things for cheap . . . and making a lot of money, and all of us living in the same house. And not exactly feeling great about it."

Gorder also points out that some of *Trading Space*'s predecessors, such as *This Old House* and *Martha Stewart Living*, mainly showed projects that were accomplishable only for people who had millions of dollars or hours of free time to spend weaving a basket on a whim.

"Americans at that time . . . didn't think they deserved beautiful things," she says. *Trading Spaces* encouraged people to think differently.

And there was a "They Loved It" compilation, too, on the Viewers' Choice DVD, with contestants gushing over a zebra-themed room and others adoring a Mexican-inflected makeover. One woman squeals and nearly goes supersonic, screaming, with joy when she sees her redone room.

From the perspective of the 2020s, the show seems to belong to another era. The worst thing its villains ever do is pour some sand on the floor of a basement to create a beach, and there was no social media where riled-up fans could hound anyone who angered them on the show—a more innocent time. But the era was still brimming with anxieties that ran deep.

The show was a kind of makeover show, a genre that goes back to *Glamour Girl*, a show that premiered in 1953. On it, women were made over with the help of consumer products, and the best makeover was decided by audience applause. It was a riff on a more successful show called *Queen for a Day*, which started on the radio in 1945 before moving to TV in 1956.

On *Queen for a Day*, women told hard-luck stories to studio audiences, whose applause determined which of the women would become queen and win products that would "solve" their problems. "Misery shows" such as *Queen for a Day* focused on contestants who were in some way disadvantaged. Women came to the show from bad circumstances, the worse the better, within limits—producers shied away from anyone who talked about rape or abuse.

Audiences ate the show up.

Queen for a Day sold a fantasy that consumer products could solve a person's problems. Producers chose contestants who "needed" something potential advertisers could provide—cookware, perhaps, or even artificial limbs—and threw in bonus prizes, revealed in infomercial-like splendor. One episode was egg-themed. All the women were somehow related to the egg business, and in addition to winning a set of new appliances, a canopy bed, and a trip to Hawaii to pick out a set of muumuus, the episode's queen won a year's supply of eggs—nevermind that many of the contestants were married to chicken farmers. It's a strange show; eggs aside, the host's auctioneer perkiness butts up oddly against the timidity of the contestants with their sob stories. I can't imagine what it must have been like to get on stage and talk about your dying son, only to have some fast-talking man cut to a commercial for Heartland Chickens or whatever.

It has a kind of hallucinatory mashup fitting for a generation enjoying a newfound imperial splendor while waiting for the bomb that would end it all.

Audiences of *Queen for a Day* got to experience a multitude of pleasures: They could feel consoled about their own positions, assuming they were better off than the people on the show; they could feel superior to others as they judged, along with the audience, which wretch was most deserving; they could feel camaraderie, cheering along with a crowd for their pick to be queen. Suffusing it all was the pleasure of succumbing to the increasingly pervasive notion that buying physical objects could solve emotional problems. In the postwar economic boom, American advertisers roared with the message that all you needed was a vacuum or a new car to feel happy, or maybe a bigger house with an in-ground pool or an unending supply of eggs.

More recent makeover shows were more extreme. Typically, they focused less on backstories and more on bodies. On *Extreme Makeover*, people got, yes, extreme makeovers, which often involved plastic surgery and untenably intense exercise regimens that supposedly transformed contestants' lives, partially by helping them conform to beauty norms. That show started in 2002 and was at the head of a wave of similar shows: *I Want a Famous Face* on MTV, *The Biggest Loser* on NBC, and *The Swan* on Fox all began in 2004. The latter was perhaps the most spectacular of the bunch. On it, "ugly" people underwent dizzying suites of plastic surgeries along with therapy and personal training appointments, then competed in a beauty pageant against each other, where they were ogled and evaluated by a panel of judges and the audience at home. It's hard to wrap your head around from the perspective of the 2020s, but audiences at the time had been primed for this kind of brutal approach to bodies.

The 2000s shows followed what media scholar Jon Dovey called the "trauma TV" of the 1990s, which focused on bodily accidents—shows such as TLC's reality show *Trauma: Life in the E.R.*, which featured doctors and nurses responding to emergencies and showed gruesome surgeries.

The media theorist Anna McCarthy called 2000s reality TV "a neoliberal theater of suffering." It was a moment when social safety nets had been gutted, and it was left for TV producers to save the suffering. For the disadvantaged, hope became privatized, and home makeover shows dramatized the chance blessings that market forces could provide. Despite the optimistic outlook that these shows had of their participants' futures, they required abject starting points. Even the cheeriest feel-good shows needed a bit of misery.

After the turn of the century, makeover shows expanded their focus from bodies and homes. *Supernanny* and *Nanny 911* remade families; *Pimp My Ride* redid cars. Even *American Idol* was a makeover show of sorts, turning amateur singers into professional stars. Anything is possible in the land of opportunity and minimal social support.

In *The Great American Makeover*, Melissa Crawley writes about the deep roots of the makeover impulse in the United States, where Europeans have long come to turn themselves into someone new. In the nineteenth century, American idols such as Henry David Thoreau, Walt Whitman, and Ralph Waldo Emerson romanticized the idea that free men could become whatever they wanted to be with a little effort and the right approach. That sensibility coexisted with Evangelical Christianity, which focused on being "born again." In a sense, the historian Clay Motley has posited, being born again is the ultimate makeover.

Religious awakenings have been central to Christianity since it began. In order to begin, the young religion relied on conversions to the belief that Jesus Christ was the son of God and savior of the world, and Jesus himself had to realize his own status before a religion was built around him. But the most vivid account of the spiritual makeovers central to early Christianity comes from one of the world's first memoirs: Saint Augustine's *Confessions.*

"How delectably it happened, all of a sudden: all of those inane delectations weren't there any longer," Augustine writes. "Now my mind was free from the gnawing anguish around advancing myself toward everything I itched for, and acquiring it, and wallowing in it, and scraping off the scabs. I prattled to you, my glory, my riches, my rescue, my Master and God."

On *Trading Spaces,* the Love It and Hate It! reveals often start similarly. The contestants open their eyes in their new rooms and look around silently, perhaps letting out an "Oh my God" or two before their shepherd, Paige Davis, asks them to clarify: Are they happy? Do they like it? And then the reactions fly.

"Hardly knowing where I was or what I was doing, I sprawled under a fig tree and gave my tears free rein," Augustine writes. "Rivers of them burst out of my eyes . . . and I spoke to you at length, not in these exact words, but in this general sense: 'But you, Master—how long? . . . Why can't *this* hour be the end of the disgusting state I'm in?'"

Embedded in Augustine's question is the underlying promise of the reveal: that something in life will become better than it was before. *Trading Spaces* "really was about change," Davis tells me. "Can you give over control and can you get something you would've never thought of on your own? And how will you take it?" How will you feel when your time comes?

Davis tells me how she got a little frustrated when she saw Crying Pam break down and her husband complain that their whole room was different. "It was very hard for me not to say, well, duh! . . . like, what did you think was gonna happen? I had to just dig really deep and tap into the compassion for two people who were not prepared emotionally to come back to a room that was so different."

Davis explains of Crying Pam: "She was not prepared for change."

—

Crying Pam might have been sensational by *Trading Spaces* standards, but her breakdown was hardly remarkable compared to the spectacles that followed on TLC.

The channel subtly began a tonal shift in the aughts by leaning into documentary-style reality shows. *Miami Ink*, a workplace comedy following life in a Florida tattoo parlor, started in 2005. *Little People, Big World* premiered the next year, following an Oregon couple with dwarfism and their children. It's a pretty quiet show that portrays the family in a sympathetic light and only ended in 2024. *Say Yes to the Dress*, the show about brides selecting wedding dresses at Kleinfeld Bridal, started in 2007 and is still running. All pretty low-stakes stuff. The same year brought *Jon & Kate Plus 8* and the next, *17 Kids and Counting*, both of which followed in the steps of *Little People, Big World* by documenting non-normative families—both of the new shows focused on families with a lot of children and started out innocuously enough. The programming still had a tenuous claim to the channel's original "learning" mission, but what followed pretty much let that go.

I Didn't Know I Was Pregnant, which focused on people who, as the title suggests, didn't know they were pregnant until they gave birth, sometimes in toilets, premiered in 2009. Unlike the previous docu-style shows that followed families over years and explored complex relationships within them, *I Didn't Know I Was Pregnant* cycles through person after person living through perhaps the biggest body horror possible: a surprise human erupting from one's body, like the xenomorph in the sci-fi horror movie *Alien*. Also in 2009, *Toddlers & Tiaras* started following colorful characters in the child pageant circuit, already an exploitative environment. The next year brought *Hoarding: Buried Alive* and *My Strange Addiction*, which portrayed people who compulsively ate cat fur and toilet paper or fell in love with their car. More unconventional body and family shows arrived and took off: *Sister Wives* began in 2010 and follows a polygamous family; *My 600-lb Life* started in 2012 and follows people who usually weigh in at 600-plus pounds; *90 Day Fiancé* started in 2014 and follows international couples marrying within the time limit allowed by the US K-1 marriage visa. They're all still running, and the latter has launched a galaxy of spin-offs that gives *Surreal Life* a run for its money (*90 Day Fiancé: Happily Ever After?*, *90 Day Fiancé: Before the 90 Days*, *90 Day Fiancé: The Other Way*, etcetera).

Around 2014, the whiff of exploitation in the air turned rancid when claims of sexual abuse surfaced involving one of the *17 Kids and Counting* kids and the boyfriend of Mama June Shannon of *Here Comes Honey Boo Boo*, a *Toddlers & Tiaras* spin-off. TLC became a slightly lurid channel, Paige Davis's perky bob a distant memory.

Trading Spaces ended in 2008. Producers had been fiddling with the show's format for a few years, at one point firing Davis and trying to go hostless before hiring her back, and trying special episodes, like featuring a divorced couple redesigning each other's bedrooms.

"They tried to Hollywood it," Wilson says of the way the producers tried to add new gimmicks and celebrity guests. "They didn't understand the wholesomeness of what we had."

At its end, *Trading Spaces* was competing with one of its behemoth children, *Extreme Makeover: Home Edition*, ABC's hit spin-off of *Extreme Makeover* that Ty Pennington went on to host. That show took the emotional stakes of *Trading Spaces* and, with the visceral intensity of the body makeover shows, raised them to the moon with family stories that didn't tug on the heartstrings so much as yank them. Families on the show had lost members to disaster, wars, and accidents, and with a giant network budget, the show didn't just renovate rooms for them over a weekend; it built entirely new homes. *Extreme Makeover: Home Edition* left *Trading Spaces* in the dust.

TLC did keep running at least one home makeover show for a bit, but audiences would rather watch someone eat fur, or so the channel's executives seemed to think. *Trading Spaces* came back for two years, starting in 2018, with Davis and a similar format and many of the same designers, but it didn't capture national attention in the same way it had originally.

Ironically, just a couple of years after TLC pulled the plug on *Trading Spaces* the first time and deemphasized the home improvement game, HGTV surged to success with that genre.

HGTV, which had long languished in the background and watched TLC eat its lunch (HGTV was offered *Trading Spaces* originally but passed on it), found zeitgeisty hits with *Property Brothers* in 2011 and *Fixer Upper* and *Flip or Flop* in 2013. The channel was no longer spouting gentle guidance about how to gussy up your castle like it had in the '90s, but something new and slightly ruthless: a torrent of professionals raising property values. These shows still focus on home beautification, but through the lens of real estate valuation, something antithetical to *Trading Spaces* and its idiosyncratic, impractical designs.

The focus on real estate began with *House Hunters,* which started on HGTV in 1999 and has since metastasized with myriad spin-offs. Of the main show alone, there have been more than 2,000 episodes. It's a straightforward real estate show: Homebuyers look at several potential properties and choose one. There are price considerations, and there is a reveal for the audience of which home the buyer chose, but there's no renovation.

Jennifer Davidson and Tara Sandler, the creators of *House Hunters*, tell me that the narrative structure of the show, which creates a guessing game for audiences about which home the buyers will choose, came from their work on '90s TLC shows. Documentary-style programs such as *A Baby Story* or *A Wedding Story* followed people going through the personal process identified in the show's title, leading to some grand result—a baby or marriage.

Davidson tells me that they realized people were watching to see what big thing was going to happen at the end of the show—the birth or wedding or whatever. She and Sandler hypothesize that part of *House Hunters'* appeal is its familiar format, repeated thousands of times: "Goldilocks and the Three Bears over and over again," she says.

The couple's inspiration came from their own search for a home in the late '90s, and a flood of HGTV real estate followed in the show's wake years later when many others in the United States had to search for new homes as well. *Property Brothers*, *Fixer Upper*, and *Flip or Flop* hit after the 2008 mortgage crisis, when the norm of middle-class homeownership in the country wobbled. On these shows and the many that followed, the makeover fantasy intertwined with real estate logic as though a mortgage broker's whispers are always fluttering in a producer's ear. On *Property Brothers* the titular siblings, Jonathan and Drew Scott, a contractor and realtor respectively, guide people through the process of buying and renovating a home. The premise is that people want a nicer home than they can afford, and the brothers help people deduce how they can make their dollar go farther by buying and redoing a fixer-upper. *Fixer Upper* takes a different tack. On it, Chip and Joanna Gaines renovate distressed properties in Waco, Texas, in a relentless modern farmhouse style that recreates an idealized, whitewashed version of the area's past: farm sinks, barn doors, and acres of shiplap. *Flip or Flop* starred Tarek El Moussa and Christina Haack, who would buy homes for cheap, often foreclosures, and renovate them for resale at a profit. The couple started doing it after the 2008 crisis in one of its epicenters, Orange County, California, and Davidson and Sandler produced the show.

The focus of these shows shifted away from the residents blessed by the miracle of production crews to the professionals engineering the designers, contractors, investors, and real estate agents overseeing the transactions. The hosts became stars of sorts, and now their televisual progeny cover the channel: *Home Town* takes the *Fixer Upper* conceit of local renovations to small-town Mississippi; *Renovation Aloha* takes it to Hawaii; *Windy City Rehab* to Chicago; *Bargain Block* to Detroit; *Bargain Block New Orleans*—you get the idea. The Gaineses even launched their own network, Magnolia, which replaced the older DIY Network, where HGTV's Duvall had fled. Humble crafts became another casualty of the real estate market.

There's not much that's humble about HGTV now. One of its marquee shows is an all-stars face-off called *Rock the Block*, where makeover meets real estate meets competition and various hosts compete against each other by finishing nearly identical spec homes in weekly challenges, adding amenities and features that sometimes feel picked from a McMansion wish list. One week they finish the kitchens, the next the primary suites; one pair will blow out a wall and add a golf simulator, another will build in a cold plunge. The final winner is the team that creates the house with the highest appraisal value. Ty Pennington hosts.

Davidson and Sandler say that the focus on financials on real estate TV evolved throughout the twenty-first century. At its dawn, it was impolite to talk too much about money, and there were no widely accessible real estate websites where you could look up how much your neighbor's house was worth. The heady days of the precrash bubble changed that. People started to talk frankly about home prices because they were climbing so outrageously. Zillow launched in 2006, letting people snoop on their neighbors' home prices. Then the mortgage crisis had people riding the real estate market like a roller coaster, and the topic of money was a star attraction.

The flipping shows came a few years after the mortgage crisis, and a morbid craze for flipping ensued, sifting through the ashes of the foreclosure storm for bones to polish and sell.

Though these real estate shows have some of *Trading Spaces*'s peppiness, the flipping aspect brings with it gloomy specters, among them the threat of unacknowledged gentrification that Adrienne Brown remarked on—wealthy white people buying the homes of Black people and other people of color and pricing them out of the areas they've historically lived in.

A newer generation of real estate shows complicated the gentrification formula as though in response to this line of criticism. HGTV's *Buying Back the Block* tweaked the format by having comedian Mike Epps and his wife, Kyra, renovate six homes on the Indianapolis block that Mike grew up on and once got evicted from. He says he wants to "make sure people can afford 'em" but doesn't get into specifics.

The show ran for only two episodes, and it didn't totally escape the problems of its predecessors. It still presented private solutions to public issues: one couple trying to remedy what a racist nation of millions did for hundreds of years.

Without government social welfare programs that organize the resources of an entire population, it's as though all that's left is for benevolent individuals to bless others as they see fit.

Trading Spaces democratized design, *Extreme Makeover: Home Edition* gave people new homes, *Buying Back the Block* highlighted the restoration of Black homeownership after racist displacement. But the extent of these shows' accomplishments exposes the limits of the societies that created them. Although these shows don't disavow public solutions, they don't mention the possibility of them, either. They rely on the power of the individualistic makeover fantasy to create an outsize emotional reaction in its audience, a kind of revival of religious hope while not actually encouraging the audience to pursue change outside the show. There are no how-to reclamation tips, no DIY decolonization of the home. Shows such as *Home Edition* and *Buying Back the Block* seem to suggest that social problems are being taken care of by do-gooders with the necessary financial means. Makeover shows suggest that changing your own home decor will lead to larger meaningful change. Reality TV can do good and inspire its audience to do nothing.

Reinvention has been part of the American experience since the first Europeans arrived. The continual colonization of land provides new opportunities to "start fresh" and forget what came before, to be born again. A more recent show on HBO Max, *Breaking New Ground*, tried to rework the theater of suffering into something more celebratory. It featured Robert Hartwell, a Broadway multihyphenate and a gay Black man, renovating a historic house in western Massachusetts. The show comes from the production company of *Property Brothers*'s Drew and Jonathan Scott. Their website says, "This series brings a new meaning to the home renovation 'reveal.'"

On the show, Hartwell explores the potential history of enslaved people who might have worked in the home while decorating it in bright colors and florid patterns and remarking on the significance of a queer Black family inhabiting the home. He wears sequined suits, animal print suits, a matching toile shirt and pant set, ostrich feathers.

It's an example of what the media scholar John Hartley has dubbed DIY citizenship, or "self-fashioning through consumerism." I buy therefore I am, and in turn I package myself as a distinctive and attractive product. This, supposedly, will release us from suffering of being overlooked by any caring society or god.

"I want you to step into this space like your crown has been straightened," Hartwell says of the interior of his soon-to-be-renovated home.

Anna McCarthy described *Extreme Makeover: Home Edition* as a neoliberal public service offering compensation for wounded souls.

"*Extreme* really was a miracle show," Pennington tells me.

Even when makeover shows focus on homes, something external to human bodies, they emphasize internal transformations.

"This is our chance to start again," a voice sings in *Home Edition's* introduction.

The overwhelming emotion of the reveal is the goal of the renovated home, a reveal of a new way of being, a break with the past that doesn't solve old problems but promises a fresh start, a new world for a new way of being. The 2000s mortgage crisis did not threaten the American Dream of homeownership so much as intensified the obsession with real estate in a nation borne of colonists pinning their hopes on a new home to start life anew.

Cruel homes offer the promise of change—and not just a single change in life, but the ability to change over and over again with every new flip in a landscape drained of culture or any sense of belonging. Hybrid homes give audiences a taste of that pleasure of reinvention even if they can't afford it. These shows aren't instructional; they offer an emotional progression that's older than America and continues to lead it down a dispiriting path.

"Why can't *this* hour be the end of the disgusting state I'm in?" begs Saint Augustine; Paige Davis says, "Open your eyes."

Let your freak flag fly

Before any pioneer woman could dream of making herself over and being born again, her ancestors had to dream about leaving their homes and escaping to somewhere better. This is the older promise that underlies the cruelty of Americans' homes and continues to shape hybrid homes today.

Escapees end up bringing the baggage of their abandoned homes with them, letting it spoil the new land and turning it into a good home for no one. It's a pattern shared by strange bedfellows: Puritans and gay guys and anyone else who has ever sought freedom on a remote coast. And while there are plenty of opportunities to study the ill effects of colonialism on the colonized, hybrid homes offer the chance to look at the ill effects of colonialism on the colonizers.

"Western civilization has a cancerous appearance; rather than transforming values, it seems intent on destroying them." The theologian Vine Deloria Jr. wrote this in *The Metaphysics of Modern Existence,* a book in which he flips the script on Western writers who have waxed poetic and mythologized Native American cultures by making sweeping generalizations about them. Instead, Deloria, a member of the Standing Rock Sioux Tribe, takes a sweeping look at Western culture, trying to understand where exactly it went wrong.

While sticking a thumb in the eye of Western science, Deloria tries to think through how the world can heal from the colonial cancer. He is suspicious of any way of thinking that attempts to establish and enforce an overarching form for how humanity should be organized, no matter how idealistic it might be.

Utopias end up focusing on their utopian ideals rather than the real lives of the people involved and the world around them. He warns against "making particular cultural traditions an absolute standard of truth, even with the best of intentions." Part of what he's saying is that he's skeptical of both capitalism and communism, along with any other ideology that sacrifices the world on the altar of an artificial social system.

Deloria sees the root of the Western problem going back to the major world faiths that focus on individual salvation or enlightenment instead of the wellness of societies and the worlds in which they exist. He's critical of any situation in which religion becomes an abstract ideal organization, disconnected from nature. Rather than continuing to try to produce transcendental utopias, involving a god or not, he thinks people should embrace their role as part of the natural world. He points out that the supposedly "primitive" societies that Europeans colonized may not have conquered the world, but they didn't destroy it either, nor did they isolate individuals and overwhelm them with incomprehensible bureaucracy.

It's the split between people and their place that Deloria identifies at the core of Western traditions that launched us toward hybrid homes. After societies decided that a theoretical metaphysical world was more important than the physical one, concrete reality was no longer enough to make a person whole. They needed something else, some reality-plus, that could give their life more.

Now that many people in America aren't looking to God and heaven to provide the added layer of existence, media and markets are there to take advantage of this cruel yearning and what people are willing to give to try to satisfy it.

People unmoored are free to wander and search new lands for the love or property or whatever else they think will make them feel whole. This untethering enables the whole colonial enterprise.

But what do people think they'll find on distant beaches that will so magically make things better?

There are clues in the almost supernatural force that seems to nest at the shore, some kind of maddening power.

"The sea! The sea!" the ancient Greek soldiers in Xenophon's history famously shouted when they caught sight of the water after months of crossing desert and mountains. They were ecstatic. The sea, they knew, would take them home.

I'm not a big beach person, and I've never wandered Anatolia after a failed military mission to usurp the Persian throne, so the shore has never brought me quite that much joy, but I might just be the oddball. For decades, American spring breakers have taken ecstatically to the shore to escape their homes, thrilled to find salvation from the strictures of their schools and jobs, free to bump and grind for hours just steps from the glittering waves. And since at least the 1990s, cameras have been there to watch. MTV shows such as *Spring Break* and *Beach House* reproduced this hedonistic pleasure space in living rooms across the country. "The sea! The sea!" a spellbound teen might exclaim, seeing freedom from domestic mores beckoning them to explore.

A lot of reality TV has been made at the beach since *Survivor* set up cameras off the coast of Borneo. For the handful of seasons in which *The Real World* didn't shoot in a city, it took place on beaches in Hawaii, Key West, and elsewhere. The shore is where Joe Francis watched girls go wild and decided to, in his words, invent reality TV. The beach is the opposite of a home setting in many ways. On the shore, restrictions on behavior are lifted. People get drunk, laze in the sun, treat each other as sexual objects, running around in little more than their underwear.

Beaches are strange places. "Ocean beaches front extraordinary vastness, opening on encompassed vistas that at first surprise, then unnerve, then bore and bore and bore," writes landscape historian John Stilgoe in *Alongshore*. Where else do people regularly walk barefoot outside? Sand underfoot creates unstable ground. Beaches literally put people off balance.

The sea itself also makes the land around it strange. Coasts defy methods of mapping and control. Long before global warming and melting ice caps led to rising seas and coastal floods, American shores were treacherous to colonial navigators who didn't know the patterns of the local land and water. Barrier islands break and drift with the tides over seasons. Sandbanks rise up out of the water one year only to disappear the next after the annual churn. Hurricanes, massive American storms "beyond European knowing," as Stilgoe puts it, crashed into coastal colonies, delivering a level of natural devastation that was only legendary in England or Spain.

Partly because they were so exposed to the elements, shores were often sparsely settled by Anglos and were lands apart for the early industrializing United States. In the 1830s, summer visitors began to descend on Eastern beaches to escape the heat of their urban homes. The salt air was supposed to be good for health, and convalescents came, boarding in private homes. By the 1850s early railroads brought travelers to hotels on the shore. Train access expanded after the Civil War, and in places such as coastal New England, visitors took hikes along the coast, bathed in the surf, and enjoyed entertainment at their hotels.

The underdeveloped shore was quaint, moving with its own natural rhythms and radiating a preindustrial charm. It was a way to step out of not only the city, but time and the logic of daily life.

"Here is ocean in all its grandeur and beauty and terror. Here disease is baffled, and death (except by shipwreck) is unknown," reads an 1878 Long Island Railroad pamphlet advertising the shores of Fire Island east of New York City.

The shore is an exceptional space of possibility. Civilization breaks down here beneath an unknowable liquid mass. To see the sea on-screen is to visualize the limits of reality.

"That's the point of being out here," Patrick McDonald says of Fire Island in the 2017 gay reality show named for the place. "Let loose, let your guard down, kind of let your freak flag fly."

It's a winning sentiment, but, coastal killjoy that I am, after watching McDonald say those words when the show came on after *Drag Race* at a viewing party at a Brooklyn bar, I probably turned to my friend and suggested we call it a night. *Fire Island* wasn't for me or for very many other people, either.

Unlike the other shows mentioned in this book, *Fire Island* did not change the nature of reality TV. It came and went in one season, and it pretty much got attention only from gay outlets, but it did, admirably, try to do something new. Unlike earlier shows, it didn't feature gay people only to humiliate them, as did the 2003 Bravo dating show *Boy Meets Boy*, which starred a gay bachelor dating a group of guys, not knowing that some of the men were straight and would win a prize if they successfully deceived him. Unlike *Drag Race*, *Fire Island* parodied nothing, attempting instead a sort of queer earnestness by documenting a group of supposed friends, including McDonald, sharing a summer beach house in an area that has for decades been a popular gay destination: the Pines on Fire Island.

The Pines is a weird place, but it's an exemplary shore destination. For decades, it's been a legendary gay getaway with no cars or businesses or seemingly any of the other trappings of modern urban life, just beautiful homes swathed in a coastal woodland where homos of all ages can flirt and fuck and do whatever else gay people want to do in their own version of domestic bliss in the private seclusion that Fire Island offers overall. Ostensibly, the show invited people into this relatively remote escape.

Fire Island is a barrier island on Long Island's southern shore, a skinny strip of land about thirty-two miles long and about half a mile wide at its widest. Today, it is mostly accessible by ferries that cross the bay between it and Long Island and stop in one of the hamlets that dot the strip, seemingly worlds away from the megalopolis to the west.

The island's history as a resort began in 1855 when the Surf Hotel opened at the western edge of island, followed by the Perkinson Hotel to the east in what is now Cherry Grove.

Cherry Grove became the first queer section of Fire Island in the 1930s, when gay writers such as W. H. Auden and Christopher Isherwood and Paul Cadmus, Jared French, and Margaret French of the artist collective PaJaMa hung out there. The enclave had a bohemian air; plenty of people who spent time there worked in theater in New York. The Great New England Hurricane of 1938, one of the most destructive storms ever to hit the United States, devastated Cherry Grove. Many left the little village, and it came back gayer.

At this point the Pines was just a stretch of empty beach, the domain of nudists and squatters just east of the Grove. But in 1952, a developer created 600 lots measuring sixty feet by a hundred feet, just over a tenth of an acre, and sold them for $800 each. The developer marketed the Pines parcels to families, not gays, and for a while there was nothing particularly queer about the area. But Peggy Fears, a former Ziegfeld Follies showgirl, Broadway producer, and lesbian, ran the yacht club in the Pines and brought some of the Cherry Grove crowd to the area. Pretty quickly it became something of a gay paradise.

"If God were to take a ribbon of land and sand and wave His Magic Wand over it, proclaiming: 'You're beautiful!,' the result would be Fire Island Pines," writes activist and author Larry Kramer in his 1978 novel, *Faggots,* in which much of the fun of the titular gay guys takes place in the Pines. By the late '70s, the beauty of the place was not just natural. The gays had remade it in their image, building unusual homes that evolved out of the design experimentation that was happening across the island.

One designer in particular set the direction that the Pines would take: Andrew Geller, a straight architect who started working on

Fire Island in the 1950s. Geller made a name for himself by designing experimental homes such as the Hunt House, a beach home shaped like a rectangular block rotated forty-five degrees so that one long edge seemed to hover a few feet above the ground. Another was like a pair of boxes, slightly crushed so that the walls buckled and bulged, letting light in through windows at the cracked edges. It was cedar-clad sci-fi, where *Dune* characters might stay if they wanted to trade sandworms for lobster rolls.

Geller built some homes in the Pines, but another designer took the lead there. Horace Gifford, a young, tall, blond, and athletic white gay man, embraced Geller's style of geometric abstraction, designing wood-clad homes hidden among trees, but he added gay twists. Standards of Victorian domesticity were nowhere to be found in Gifford's homes. Rooms flowed into one another. Bathrooms had big windows, exposing them to the passersby on walkways outside. Instead of a sequence of formal dining and living rooms, there was often a single grand shared space surrounded by bedrooms. Walls opened up for afternoon parties to flow from sundecks to conversation pits when the sun went down. It's a rowdier version of the midcentury modernism that flourished in the Hollywood Hills, more experimental and less reflective of a *Jetsons*-esque domesticity. Gifford's first home adapted ideas from a bathhouse, the one that his mentor Louis Kahn designed in Trenton, New Jersey.

"Architecture of seduction," Christopher Rawlins calls it in *Fire Island Modernist,* a monograph of Gifford's work. The architecture critic Alastair Gordon likens the stripped-back homes that came together at odd angles or had rooms thrusting past each other to "stage sets for concealment and exposure . . . inviting voyeuristic tendencies, while indulging a taste for flamboyance."

Gifford quickly established a reputation, sometimes going to meetings in nothing but his swim suit. He worked for the new gay elite: Calvin

Klein hired Gifford to design a pool complex behind his Pines house, which David Geffen would later buy. Other architects designed similar homes that filled the Pines. As the style took over during the '70s, it got grander and more spatially eccentric, great for parties or maybe drug-fueled orgies, if that was what you wished.

Another architect named Earl Combs followed in Gifford's direction, designing a Pines home for the owner of a local restaurant in one of the most prominent locations in the neighborhood, at the oceanside end of one of the paths that cross the island. Laid out like an arc of cabana-like bedrooms around a deck with a large pool facing the sea, the home sits like a crown on the sand next to the steps that visitors take down to the beach.

A "dream house," Jorge Bustillos calls it in *Fire Island's* first episode, and when I visited the house, where the show takes place, it did feel like a dream in that it didn't follow the logic of any house that I had been in before. Grand entry stairs led straight to the middle of the home and a wall of windows, so that when I walked in, I was staring straight out at the sundeck, pool, and sky.

"This is paradise," Bustillos says about the Pines on the show, and standing in the home, it felt that way. Unfortunately, paradise has baggage.

The Pines is an escape from the mainland, a place where lifestyles and homes can take new shapes and form communities and landscapes that can't readily take root elsewhere. The Pines isn't just at the shore, it's *of* the shore, a fruit of the beach's ability to reorient people to new horizons and offer a hidden place on the fringe. But though the shore's on the edge, it's not quite somewhere else. It may have a view of the psychotic sea, but it's still held back by the hinterland.

The Pines, despite all its exciting possibilities, is as snobbishly exclusive as places come. It's a snobbery that's baked into its buildings, which is clear when you look at its neighbor and forebear, Cherry Grove.

Cherry Grove is also gay, but the houses there are generally more traditional American coastal homes, simple and wooden, more like what you'd find in other seaside towns on the Atlantic.

The narrator of Kramer's *Faggots* puts it: "The Pines is newer, classier, and more expensive and amusing, and has better shops and handsomer, younger, more affluent fellows, and bigger houses, more tastefully decorated, and for all these reasons the older and less stylishly oriented go to Cherry Grove."

The major architectural accent of Cherry Grove is the work of a retail display designer named John Eberhardt, who in 1956 built the Belvedere Guest House. It's a little palace, decked out with curlicues and urns, guarded by ornamental lions and watched over by a cupola-topped tower. "Architecture in drag," Rawlins calls it.

Early on, the Pines didn't have the gay reputation that its neighbor had, making it a safer destination for anyone who wanted to stay closeted at work or wherever else. Cherry Grove, with its frilly guest house, stood for a florid working-class femininity with no boardroom aspirations. The Pines was home to a certain kind of status-conscious gay man attached to masculinity and other markers of success in the wider world, Calvin Kleins and David Geffens with appetites that did not necessarily align with the idea of a queer haven, much less utopia. It became a modern place for an emerging gay elite.

"A sassy, sprawling nouveau-riche community," gay rights activist Jack Nichols wrote about the Pines in 1976. "Decadent, dumb, and lovely."

Gifford designed forty homes total in the Pines, but none in Cherry Grove.

The modernist experiments of the Pines were not visions of traditional domesticity, but they also weren't bohemian homes encouraging new ways of living. They are their own kind of drag, a butch one without any lacy frills and just the stripped, hard flesh of buildings stretching beneath the sun.

In the Pines the charming walkways winding through trees don't foster treehouse-like whimsy so much as Beverly Hills-esque seclusion. Luxury and privacy go hand in hand—Rawlins tells me that people started putting in pools around 1970, and building codes required fences around them. The fences started getting larger, leading to a "creeping suburbanization of taste," as he puts it, that transformed the areas. The walkways of the Pines now often don't even lead directly to front doors. Gates have sprung up, blocking access to houses from the walkways that serve as public pedestrian streets, keeping the riffraff far from the homes, as though they were in Hidden Hills.

But the original Pines parties started to wind down in the 1980s. Construction slowed in the area because it was largely built out by then, Rawlins says. After residents across the island banded together to resist plans for a highway across the island put forward by Robert Moses, the legendary New York powerbroker and planner, the federal government established the Fire Island National Seashore in '64, which left only so much room to grow. Where the expressway didn't burn through, AIDS did. Combs died in '91, and Gifford in '92. Now, much of the Pines seems frozen in time, at least architecturally.

On *Fire Island*, it's as though the place is being rediscovered. Some of the roommates are new to the Pines, and the sexuality on display there shocks many of them. Freak flag McDonald is the only local; he works there as a bartender and lives there full-time, so when the others go back to the city during the week, he stays. Unlike his roommates, who are often in button-downs or simple T-shirts and shorts, McDonald wears speedos and what he calls "scrop tops," a portmanteau of "skank tanks" and crop tops. He calls his style "trailer trash hot." On the first episode, he invites his local friends to a day party at the house. One gets naked by the pool, igniting Bustillos.

"My house is not a strip club," Bustillos says, and launches into a tirade. "This is a family barbecue . . . it is about people and manners."

Later, the castmates have a house meeting to debrief and roommate Cheyenne Parker talks about how "they probably want to keep the image of the household up." They agree to be more careful about who they invite to the house, and I roll my eyes at how lame a group of gay guys manages to be.

Over the course of the season, McDonald butts heads with the others, many of whom seem to look down on McDonald and his local friends who live and work on Fire Island for the summer, presumably in service jobs. The show does not talk about class explicitly, but it's there in coded conversations about image and behavior, the same concerns that have driven the Pines to hypermasculine drag, perfect for displaying a life of success.

I sympathize more with McDonald, but only because he's the poor outcast of the group who's not afraid to live a little, not because he's so gung ho about the Pines. I've been iffy about the area for as long as I've lived in New York City. For all its fantasy of fun, sex, and gay ol' times, it's always been redolent of a certain version of hell: Instagram posts of sun-soaked rich white professionals and poseurs sharing bedrooms rented at exorbitant rates, captions extolling "community" and the magic of a place that runs on exclusivity, pink capitalism, and credit card debt. It reminded me of everything I couldn't afford throughout my twenties, when I barely had $1000 to spend on a surgery my insurance wouldn't cover, much less on a weekend—a weekend!—in a share house. Instead I stayed home, looking for less invasive ways of dealing with an overgrown keloid.

I know I'm not alone in feeling disenchanted with gay utopia. Yes, there's a book by photographer Tom Bianchi of 1970s and '80s Polaroids that show lithe white men canoodling poolside in the Pines that haunts Brooklyn living rooms like a gay version of the LIVE, LAUGH, LOVE sign, but there are also people such as Shawn Escarciga, aka @missladysalad on X, who created a meme in May 2024 with the words "Gosh I love that

June is almost here." In the image, beneath the words "Never lose sight of the power of community," is the facade of a modernist house behind a sandy yard with four raw chicken breasts and one whole raw chicken sans feet and head posed in front of it. The slabs of meat have text in front of them: "I'm a gay landlord!" reads one; "I'm a gay war profiteer!" says the one next to it. The others: "I'm a gay for-profit doctor!" "I'm a gay gallery owner!" And the last, in the background: "I'm just rich but also a gay genocide denier!" Two are in ball caps, one from Goldman Sachs, the other from Raytheon. The post got thousands of likes.

Without saying it explicitly, the meme is clearly about the Pines, largely because the house in the background is of the area's distinctive style—it's designed by Gifford and on the cover of the second edition of Rawlins's book.

The Pines really is a beautiful place. Elevated walkways wend through stands of scrappy barrier island trees to wood-clad modernist fantasias in crystalline forms that sometimes tower on hilltops, crowned with roof terraces offering chicken breasts a chance to bake beneath the summer sun. If it weren't for all the wealth and whiteness, maybe it could be a utopia, or at least a place where another world would be possible. Whenever I've walked through those woods and sat on the long beach stretching either way to the horizon with the sun shining overhead and the ocean reaching beyond the edge of the Earth, I have been enchanted by the feeling that I've fallen out of time and escaped whatever was bothering me in my life, that I had made it somewhere I had been trying to get to my whole life, some kind of paradise that was my true home. The sea! The sea! I get what those Greeks were excited for.

But like any fantasy of escape, it disappoints—something all too familiar about gay spaces, whether they be physical or on-screen.

Reality TV has been a land of opportunity for queer people compared to scripted media. When it started, reality TV was expected to be outrageous, and so gay people didn't have to be as bland and respectable as they might have to be on a weekly sitcom, if they were allowed to be there at all.

"I, RuPaul, was born a poor Black child in the Brewster housing projects of San Diego, California," a disembodied voice says over framed shots of a smiling child. "But baby . . . look at me now!" Glamour clips take the screen. "As the original supermodel of the world, I've had all my dreams come true. And now it's time for me to share the love. I'm looking for America's next drag superstar."

So began *RuPaul's Drag Race*, the first gay reality TV hit. Since its beginning on the gay-themed channel Logo in 2009, it has aired hundreds of episodes and launched franchises around the world.

From its first words, the show tells jokes that are never explained and rely on audiences to catch the references. Host of the show, drag queen RuPaul Andre Charles, did grow up in San Diego, but not in the Brewster Housing Projects. There are no Brewster Housing Projects in San Diego. There were, however, the Brewster-Douglass Projects in Detroit, Michigan, and RuPaul's idol, Diana Ross, grew up there, as serious fans of hers, Charles among them, would know. The opening lines signal that what follows is not to be totally taken seriously.

When it launched, *Drag Race* was heavy-handed in its parody of de-alienated labor competition shows such as *The Apprentice* or *America's Next Top Model*. "To win this competition, you're gonna need to be more enterprising than Donald Trump, to give bigger than Oprah, and to be hotter than Tyra wearing a fat suit in July," Charles tells contestants on the first episode. The show assumed that audiences would understand the references without explanation, along with other lightly coded messages throughout the show, such as that the contestants would be judged on their charisma, uniqueness, nerve, and talent, a phrase composing an acronym for a word that could not be said on basic cable television. (Bless my heart, it took me years to get that reference because it is never explained on the show.)

Drag Race was unlike any show that came before it. It pushed boundaries and ironically poked fun at the conventions of show business. On the first episode, the first contestant to appear, Shannel, introduces herself to the audience by saying, "people call me the Barbra Streisand of drag," as she walks around the show's set and reveals her bare butt cheeks sticking out of cutouts in her pants. Shannel explains the Streisand comparison: "I've heard she's a real bitch and she's anal retentive about everything," and Shannel says she is, too. Shannel's outfit elicits a remark from another contestant, Akashia, when she walks into the room in similarly revealing clothing: "When I saw Shannel, I was like, oh, another skank with her butt hanging out," she says in a confessional. "I thought I was gonna be the only one . . . Hers is a little flabby—it jiggles. Mine is solid muscle so it doesn't, like, move at all." After all the contestants arrive, Charles comes into the room to announce the show's prizes—causing one contestant, Ongina, to say, "I'm so excited I just drip"—and the show's first challenge: pose in a photo shoot while being sprayed with water and washing a car with two scantily clad men.

The show is absurd, but it maintains and exaggerates the traditional emotional structure of a competition: The bottom two contestants of every episode have to face a judging panel and "lip-synch for their lives," as Charles puts it with over-the-top intensity. Contestants regularly break down in hysterics when they lose. Absurdity and sincerity coexist.

"If you look below the comedy veneer, you still have the beats that work just like the beats of reality competition," Brian Graden says of the show. "You're still watching to see how they do and who wins. And so it really is the best of both worlds."

Logo was "the first twenty-four-hour network" to focus on gay content, Graden says. He helped launch it in 2005. Reality TV was a key component of the channel's early programming because it was easier to produce quickly, as when Fox was starting in the '80s, broadcasting a lot of unscripted content.

Graden says that creating just one episode of a scripted drama would've taken up their entire programming budget. And just rerunning existing shows, though it could cheaply fill time, wouldn't bring the channel a lot of attention. Original series brought press coverage and audiences, so reality was the way to go.

Drag Race was the channel's biggest hit, though it didn't seem to set out to be that. At least in the beginning, the show seemed to be scornful of success with a broader audience. "I'd rather have an enema than have an Emmy," Charles told E. Alex Jung in an interview with *Vulture* in 2016. Charles says in the same interview that drag "will never be mainstream. It's the antithesis of mainstream." Later that year, Charles won his first Emmy for hosting the show. Within a few years, it became one of the most decorated Emmy winners in reality TV.

During that time, fans criticized Charles for speaking enthusiastically about making money from fracking and saying he would "probably not" let a trans woman on the show, despite trans women having been central to drag as long as the practice has existed in its modern form. (The show has since changed its position on trans women competing on the show; no word on fracking.) Charles's gender-liberatory message of "we're all born naked and the rest is drag" was twisted to capitalist ends when he told viewers in an online course for MasterClass (subscriptions available for ten dollars per month) that if they want to make more money, they should put on a suit. A far cry from him telling Jung, "I don't think there is a life in the mundane nine-to-five hypocrisy. That's not living."

Drag Race is now a machine, churning out new seasons, spin-offs, and specials with relentless regularity. The show's humor has a gentler bite than it used to; where once there was a sudsy car-washing scene with nearly naked men, there are now pop-up appearances from the

Teletubbies, Hello Kitty, and Nancy Pelosi. Charles has won more than a dozen Emmys. He leads contestants through personal branding challenges: "You want to know who your consumer is and what they want from you, and then you want to deliver that for them," he advises in a 2022 season. Drag is a mainstream product, if controversially so. Like on *The Real Housewives*, raunch took a back seat and something like an aesthetic of respectability politics replaced it, a glorification instead of exploitation of the bodies on-screen—that is, if they played by the rules of consumer games and created nice little packages of success.

In its early years, *Drag Race* suggested an alternative path for reality TV, one that didn't chase traditional notions of success. It showed how queer culture could present alternatives to heteronormative American domesticity. Talk of chosen families and demonstrations of intergenerational friendships abounded. But like the Pines, the show has become crushed by its laurels, no longer pushing boundaries but extracting all the wealth it can from the territory it has colonized.

Over the past few years, two groups have proposed two very different paths forward for the Pines.

In late 2023, a group of gay men announced plans for a new Fire Island. Without a specific location in mind, the group was looking to replicate the Pines and build a gay neighborhood somewhere in the Mediterranean. Their idea was that they would find uninhabited land and develop it for gay men. "Target: US$500,000 for a four-bedroom freestanding house with a pool in gay paradise," the group's website read.

People criticized the plans on social media for its questionable approach, prompting a response in the organization's newsletter. After saying that the group is against gentrification if that means displacing marginalized people from their existing homes, the newsletter says that the group supports gentrification if means making the most of a real estate opportunity.

"Gay colonisation is also something we are all about if it means a majority gay population," the newsletter goes on. "Why not spend a few weeks or months a year in a 100% gay place when we spend so much of our lives in a straight world?"

Also in 2023, a different group of people doubled down on the original Pines, advocating a sort of recolonization of it.

"Doll Invasion is an annual community-led tradition galvanizing all trans people to journey en masse to Fire Island, providing access to a private pool party venue in the historically inaccessible, cisgender gaycation paradise," reads an Instagram post from the group.

The Doll Invasion follows in the steps of the annual July 4 drag invasion, when a boat full of queens pulls into the Pines's harbor while onlookers watch from the shore. Drag was one of the dividing lines between Cherry Grove and its butch neighbor. Drag queens were originally welcome only in the former; the Pines scorned them. The split between the two was so intense that in 1976, a Cherry Grove resident, Teri Warren, was refused service at a restaurant in the Pines because she was in drag. A retaliatory "invasion" began that repeats every year, though now the queens are cheered when they arrive.

The Doll Invasion may become something similar, although it seems to face some financial barriers related to hosting a house party in such an expensive location. A 2024 Instagram post solicits donations at varying scales, the top being "$5000 1/5th (dear god) of our rental price." Although the drag invasion inserted drag queens into the uptight Pines, it did not do much to change its overall elitism. It broke through the gates without tearing down the walls. The Doll Invasion's effects may be different, but I'm not holding my breath. It did get a splashy Vogue feature and a charity collab with celebrity chef Alison Roman, but it doesn't seem to take apart the place's appeal, only to want to be in the club.

And what a club it is. In his poem "Portrait of Yung Kathy #2", playwright Jeremy O. Harris describes the "dark gay path" of homosexuals with "eyes as empty as their wallets are full stomachs grumbling ravenous for something or someone new to consume." They're the chicken breasts in Escarciga's meme, looking for feed. The poem then lists a litany of global gay destinations where the hungry roam before ending with a Fire Island scene.

Colonization is as much about escaping from one place as it is about claiming another. There's fantasy involved on either end: the belief that it's possible to cleanly leave the past behind and that the new land is a blank canvas for a fresh start. Neither is ever true. Disappointment ensues for the colonizer; things are much worse for the colonized. The cycle repeats when the disappointed colonizer leaves again to find happiness. It's the same emotional rhythm that propelled Anglos to California to start new lives and fall in love in the footsteps of Ramona—the dream of the makeover, the spiritual rebirth—and it's still propelling Americans to constantly look for some new place where they can manifest a new destiny.

It's impossible to find paradise on stolen land, not so much because of any supposed specters that haunt the soil but because of the infertility of the new seeds planted there. Colonizers don't hold the potential for real life in them. Colonizers dream of death—the death of the past, of their old selves, of anyone who gets in their way.

Instead of dreaming of utopia, the poet Kyle Carrero Lopez has proposed an alternative: queering dystopia, or dealing with how messed up things are right now not by escaping them but by finding ways to make them different. He advocates twisting the systems that control us to create pockets of possibility amid the ruin.

What would that look like? The drag queen Lushious Massacr makes videos for YouTube and social media that give a taste.

Instead of selling a fantasy of a dream home, Lushious films what dreams are being sold, "dragvestigating" local home goods stores, aka picking through the crap at Ross and dd's Discounts and commenting on what's cute and what's garbage. In these videos, Lushious is not in full *Drag Race* glam. She's instead a little rough around the edges, something that she winks at when she exhorts her audience to support the "bricks" and the "non-passable dolls." She's a bit of a gender bandit, going out in public the way that she sees fit and not demurely hiding or being quiet but instead being a funny, loud asshole—but she's only really mean to IKEA and the like.

Lushious is political, often explicitly so. Before moving to LA in 2025, she lived in Brownsville, Texas, which is on the Mexican border, and she crisscrosses the dividing line between the two countries, talking about the racism and idiocy of America's border policies in many videos. In others, she talks about prejudice against trans women, mentioning at least once with a laugh how many of her predecessors didn't live very long. But she never makes tragedy porn or appeals to a pitying white audience. Instead she invites people like her to have a blast, no matter how ugly the world or the stuff at Home Goods is.

It wasn't that long ago that the only time that you'd see someone like Lushious on-screen is if she were on the news being arrested or worse. Lushious's videos are tinged with the sass of Stephanie Yellowhair, a transgender Navajo woman who appeared on an early 2000s episode of *Cops* while getting cuffed. "Excuse my beauty," she told the police, restrained, in the back of their car, securing queer icon status forever. Lushious doesn't ask to be excused, instead telling dystopia to deal with what she's got. And people love it.

Fire Island didn't find an audience. It didn't poke fun at wealth or make it ridiculous, as *The Real Housewives* or *Keeping Up With the Kardashians* did. It offered no surreal feeling of inflated importance for viewers. The show tried to make the wealth of the Pines seem normal while painting McDonald, the lone roommate who was one of the local laborers, as immoral and lascivious, in need of being reined in by the rest of the cast. It assumed its audience would enjoy a look inside an exclusive place without offering viewers any way in. It couldn't hybridize its homes, and people didn't stay.

The show is part of the ethos of a gay rights movement that worked for the right to marry and serve in the military, that celebrated representation, diversity, and inclusion in an American system without fundamentally critiquing it, that rarely talked about class as a problem within queer communities. Wealth, in this worldview, is invisible, as natural as the Pines's butch architecture, seemingly a fruit of the local landscape. It's an ethos that only went so far, running out of steam around the same time that *Fire Island* did.

Lately, the reality TV industry in general has been struggling. All of TV has been wobbly for a variety of reasons, but many of them stem from the new competition that people are carrying around with them. Phones, laptops, and other screens now offer bits of reality for free, with algorithms designed to present a content stream tailored just for you. Reality TV may have pioneered hybrid homes, but hybrid homes will go on just fine without reality TV, evolving with whatever new platform that technology provides.

This new age is scrambling some of the old hierarchies of reality TV, including geographical ones. No longer need Southern California or the shore be production hubs for video creation, now that the tools for it are in millions of hands around the world. In 2022, Khabane "Khaby" Lame, a former factory worker from the Turin area of Italy, became the most followed person on TikTok in the world, often creating videos from what seemed to be his relatively modest apartment. There are beaches everywhere for those with the eyes to see. But there's one state where the spiritual descendants of the Pilgrims are progressing: the Beehive State, which keeps alive an old American vision of paradise on Earth that resonates across the country and beyond. The future of reality goes through Utah.

Just a girl with big dreams

I love Salt Lake City. I spent the day there once. It was fall, when the leaves popped against snow-capped summits, and the spacious grid of streets hummed with the busyness of the faithful. Faces smiled at me while I toured the Mormon monuments; helpful answers came from greeters outside the Tabernacle about the daily noon organ recital, which followed a brief demonstration of the space's acoustics. Receptionists welcomed me at the Church History Museum, where I peered at recreations of Joseph Smith's golden plates and dioramas of the Mormon migration across the continent to a promised land in the mountains. At night, while I drove down Interstate 15 through the valley that the city sits in, the sober traffic flowed easily around me, as though I were a salmon in my native stream, and I looked across the landscape to see white temples shining like miniature peaks, rising up to heaven along with the blessed earth around them.

I was enthralled by Utah, and millions of others have been, too, judging from the visions of the state that have been all over my screens, from *The Real Housewives of Salt Lake City* and *The Secret Lives of Mormon Wives* and seemingly every other influencer I saw on TikTok or Instagram. But as someone who wanders inconsistently across the gender spectrum and is a lapsed Catholic who hasn't sat through a mass since my confirmation, falling in love with the place wasn't what I expected when I planned my trip.

Salt Lake City is different from Fire Island in a lot of ways—it's probably more racially diverse, for one—but I had the same world-apart feeling there, just in a setting that traded sand dunes for snowdrifts. I'm far from the first person to glimpse paradise in Utah. There are all the Mormons who trekked here more than a century ago, the pioneers who believed they were fulfilling prophesies old and new, preparing for an apocalypse they thought was soon coming with the avidity of a gay guy preparing his outfit for afternoon tea. Salt Lake City is a strange place.

But Utah is not odd because it deviates from mainstream Americanness but because it is a rare flower of ancient ideas and emotions that have shaped the country and long precede it. Up there in the thinner air, certain notions have been preserved like Alpine mummies, but these ideas are hardly dead, maybe more alive than ever, and Utah has the blueprints for the world being built around us.

—

There are plenty of places to see videos of weird and wonderful homes online: *Architectural Digest* tours of celebrity homes; social media accounts such as Zillow Gone Wild that spotlight freaky anomalies of the real estate market; and plenty of other progeny that *Cribs* and *House Hunters* have unleashed. But it's the background spaces of the viral content that social media has spawned that better reflect the hidden impulses shaping hybrid homes.

Consider this video posted on TikTok in October 2024: In a gray-and-white kitchen, a woman sets a wooden cutting board on a counter. On it, her manicured hands place a pineapple, then pears, oranges, apples, and grapes. The woman is wearing a pleated yellow dress with a translucent top layer that fans out over her body. Long sleeves splay outward, giving her the appearance of an elegant jellyfish. She keeps this outfit on during the video's next segments, showing her chopping and juicing the fruit, straining the result, and diluting it with water before pouring it into two plastic pouches for her kids to drink.

This is Nara Smith, a model and TikToker who became an internet sensation in 2024. She has just made from-scratch Capri-Sun, the children's beverage that's drunk out of little pouches in cafeterias across the country. The video has been viewed more than 50 million times, her most-watched clip of that year.

Throughout the video, Smith narrates in her signature voiceover style, a breathy stage whisper. She slightly elongates the end of every phrase with a dash of vocal fry. It's an odd way of speaking, one she has said is influenced by ASMR. Her voice, pushed to the deeper end of her register, wavers, making it sound like she might break into tears or rage, but her tone is flat and her intonation rhythmic as though she is casting a mesmeric spell—which she is, though her magic is one of modern media, not metaphysics.

"While my toddlers were playing in the backyard, they asked me for a Capri-Sun," she says at the start of the video, accenting the first syllable in the drink name in a continental fashion. "Since I had all the fruit at home to make some, I told them to give me a minute." She's matter-of-fact, making the whole operation sound natural, as though throwing on a gown and taking out the juice machine were the most obvious response to a kid's request for refreshment.

In 2024, Smith developed her formula for viral videos, whipping up homemade versions of mass-produced snacks that her husband, fellow model Lucky Blue Smith, or their young kids had ostensibly requested. She made SpaghettiOs, Froot Loops, Coca-Cola, and Lucky's favorite—Takis. She always maintains the same vocal style and narrative, but she mixes up the outfits and makes some treats she's been craving as well. In a December video, she made her favorite dessert, panna cotta with a raspberry sauce, in a scaled red $12,000 Ferragamo dress that made her look like a couture pangolin.

Every time these videos would pop up I would watch them. They weren't long, usually just a minute or so, and they came and went easily. They didn't have any shouting or overhyped "you gotta see this" introductions, just soothing little snacks on the screen.

Smith is part of the broader balm universe on social media. This is not in-your-face viral content. It's part of the internet's great boring deluge of information, the repetitive stream that washes over screens with regularity, as reliable as the tides and as banal. What runs along with it are YouTubers giving daily reviews of new eye shadows, Twitch streamers playing Fortnite for hours, Instagram reels of cats chasing their own tails. This kind of content often doesn't shout for attention; it purrs soothingly with every stroke of the phone for those weary of the volatile, liquid world. It flows easily in our current cultural medium, unobjectionable material for advertisers and algorithms to embrace.

But Smith, for all her soothingness, is strange, and that's part of her success. When she says her sister-in-law ran out of bubble gum so she decided to whip some up in the kitchen, it's a kind of rage baiting, meant to get incredulous strangers to post comments such as "WTF??" and signal to the algorithm that this content is worth boosting. It's the same tactic that Donald Trump used so successfully to get coverage of his first presidential run, casually saying something outrageous that news media would breathlessly cover as though it were sincere. Unlike Trump, who smirks at the rubes, Smith never drops her mask.

In a video she posted at the end of 2024 reflecting on the year she rocketed to fame, Smith recounts her life journey from a teenage girl "wondering what she would become" to modeling, getting married, having children, and falling in love with "intentional cooking," as she puts it.

She says of herself: "Even though what she was building came with a lot of opinions and backlash and people criticizing every step of the way, she still found herself showing up every single day not only for her but every young girl that's just a girl with big dreams." There's no winking irony here, no inside joke for her loyal followers, just the kind of navel-gazing gratitude you might see in an Oscar winner's speech.

In an interview with *Harper's Bazaar*, Smith insists that she has no hidden agendas. "I post videos of me cooking for my kids and my husband," she says. "It's really not that deep."

Smith is a development of America's villain era, a daughter of Christine Quinn and her winking outrageousness, but she also ties together several threads in influencer history: She blends the boring internet with what Sianne Ngai calls the "mass-popular style of a neoliberal, multicultural age in which performances of 'extreme identity' have become the status quo"—the drag queen in a massive bleach-blond wig and overdrawn lips selling a makeup line; the Real Housewife in a latex fetish suit recording her next single; the farmer Bachelorette contestant riding up to the mansion on a tractor; Mariah Carey exercising in heels on *Cribs*. Ngai cites a term from the artist and writer Guillermo Gómez-Peña for this: the "mainstream bizarre." These are casual displays of outré identities that have become so ubiquitous as to make the strange normal and the normal strange, products of an age when people feel the need to be seen by an audience because they're not being seen by any other system of care.

Smith also has more than a whiff of trad wife—that is, a follower of a reactionary online movement in which women espouse "traditional" gender roles, such as dressing nicely for their husbands and living to serve their men and kids. A paragon trad wife is Hannah Neeleman, who goes by @ballerinafarm online, a former dancer who married the scion of the Jet Blue fortune and now raises eight kids on a Utah ranch, where she documents herself on social media making treats such as a turmeric latte using her cows' milk straight from the udder.

Via the trad wife, Smith pulls in a few other disparate strains of digital culture. Trad wifery overlaps with what could be called Dimes Square politics, or a Biden-era craze among bored and pampered young-ish people to roll their eyes at progressive virtue signaling and instead advertise reactionary beliefs like toddlers sticking their tongues out at daycare instructions. It's a posture for people for whom critical thinking is too hard but who still crave a sort of radical chic. Picture a disaffected sigh and suppressed eye roll regarding anything sincere, an embrace of nihilistic partying and quest for attention without looking like that's what you want. Dimes Square luminaries, such as Dasha Nekrasova and Anna Khachiyan of the podcast *Red Scare*, embrace reactionary gender roles as much as they embrace anything earnestly, although they would probably never be caught milking a cow to make their latte. The Dimes Square mentality is largely urban—it's named for the section of Chinatown in New York that the group seems to gravitate toward—and has little to do with farming or cooking from scratch.

In its rural mythmaking, the trad wife movement shares more with what the journalist Emily Matchar called the New Domesticity. Matchar chronicled a fit of interest in domestic skills such as canning and knitting among young professional women around the 2008 Great Recession and how blogs and emerging social networks helped the fascination spread. It was a millennial riff on the rural fantasizing that led aspiring farmers to the San Fernando Valley and Ralph Borsodi to go back to the land. The trad wife took this nostalgia and turned it into a political position, a sort of Make Gender Great Again movement for the disaffected young woman.

Smith doesn't fit neatly into either the Dimes Square or New Domestic mold. She never mentions politics, and she doesn't totally espouse the "disconnect and drop out" mentality that Matchar saw among women taking to homemaking while the financial world crumbled around them. Smith frequently travels for photo shoots and gives interviews, very much still a part of the fashion world that she's been working in. She denies being a trad wife—"I'm not a trad wife. I'm a working mum," she told *The Times*—though she certainly skirts trad wife territory. She bends over backward to delight her husband and kids by cooking for hours and has made friends with Neeleman. Smith is at least trad wife adjacent, or perhaps she personifies an evolution of the persona toward something new, pulling together the casual provocations of Dimes Square with the belabored fantasies of a mother-cum-milkmaid toward some new destination that is apparently incredibly popular.

Wherever she's headed, Smith follows in the footsteps of her adopted faith: Mormonism.

Smith was not born into a Mormon family and converted for Lucky, who was. Still, she mimics the many pioneer women who preceded her and documented their lives in detail.

Mormons have been major bloggers for decades and diarists for longer. The Church of Jesus Christ of Latter-day Saints, or the LDS Church, is the main branch of modern Mormonism and has long encouraged journaling as a way for followers to record the influence of God in their lives, for the diarist's own edification and for that of their descendants.

The church is also constantly recruiting new members, and it encourages followers to share stories of their faith with others, partially to help win newcomers over. In the 2000s, Mormon mothers became stars of a subset of the New Domesticity movement, mommy blogging, in which mothers documented their experiences online, shared products and tips, and created global communities focused on the experience of raising kids. Fueled by the church's celebration of families and child-rearing and its desire to present an attractive appearance to potential converts, Mormons went wild.

Though Lucky occasionally talks about his faith in interviews and on social media, Nara seems to avoid the subject. Again, she doesn't fit the mold, no more a traditional Mormon mommy blogger than she is a Dimes Square dilettante or New Domestic canning peaches grown in her backyard.

Smith is more akin to a Kardashian living in a modern farmhouse, but that's not an exact match, either. The kitchen where Smith shot the videos that launched her into viral fame is not a sleek museum space where Kendall Jenner might try to cut up a cucumber. Its muted surfaces are matte or slightly shiny, nothing close to a high-gloss sheen. The kitchen also lacks traditional details; the upper cabinets in the background are unembellished gray boxes. It's not the shellacked modernism of *Selling Sunset* or the macho modernism of the Pines or a ubiquitous nostalgic style such as Mediterranean Revival. The kitchen is more remarkable for its banality: There are no personal artifacts or distinctive decorations or daring design features such as giant sliding glass walls. I could imagine living there the same way I felt I could live in Salt Lake City. Why not? But the kitchen of Smith's 2024 videos didn't even have that Beehive State charm—Smith does not live in Utah. She was born in South Africa, grew up in Germany, and decided to move to Dallas in 2022 with Lucky ("in search of a clean slate and a way to save on state income tax," she says in a 2024 *GQ* profile) before buying a house in Connecticut at the end of '24. The content that shot her to fame was recorded in her Texas home. It's a generic gray space, the personality-less kind that could be a luxury interior anywhere in the world.

But there's something pleasantly boring about Smith's gray space's lack of high contrast black-and-white patterns or bright colors, something soothing about it. There's no messiness to it, none of the roughness of nature. It's just as predictable as Smith's repetitive narrative format. It's always perfectly clean, a brand-new product in every scene. Smith doesn't use any folksy cast-iron pots or pans; everything is nonstick, covered in a hexagonally patterned skin. Her cutting board is wood, but it's a glued-together slab that turns the grain into an abstracted grid of stripes. Like the eye-numbing gray interiors of spec condos, fast-casual restaurants, and so much of the rest of the world being built today, Smith's kitchen is unabashedly artificial. And in that, I learned, these spaces are similar to a classic Mormon aesthetic.

Mormonism began in an area of western New York State known as the "burned-over district" for the intensity of the religiosity that swept through during the early nineteenth-century's Second Great Awakening, a time of spiritual revival in the United States when crowds flocked to hear preachers speak. In 1820, a teenage boy named Joseph Smith went to the woods not far from his upstate home to ask God which of the many religious sects flaming in the area he should follow. He had a vision. Two divine beings told him that all the sects were wrong. He was later visited by the angel Moroni, who showed Smith in a vision golden plates covered with a strange script, which Smith found and translated using "seer stones" to produce the Book of Mormon, named for Moroni's father, an ancient prophet who supposedly wrote much of the Golden Plates text. The book was an additional volume of Christian scripture describing a journey of Jesus in the Americas after his resurrection, where he established the church that the Mormons were to revive. This was way the to the truth. The spirited young Smith started preaching and built a following. He founded the Church of Jesus Christ of Latter-day Saints in 1830 in the New York town of Fayette, then fled, escaping persecution, first to Ohio, then to Missouri, then Illinois, where he died. Brigham Young, Smith's successor, finally led the flock to Utah, then a remote area for Anglo settlers. There, the LDS Church set about creating a holy land of sorts in preparation for the apocalypse and return of Christ to Earth.

The apocalypse is a big deal to Mormons, an orienting feature for both faith and life, as it was for many Christians during the Second Great Awakening. At the time, many were obsessed with connecting the references scattered throughout the Bible to the end of the world, and they developed a sort of science that attempted to decode mentions of signs and symbols. Theorists developed a timeline of events that would precede the end of the world and started to see these events happening around them, not unlike a conspiracy theorist "proving" in a YouTube video how Democrats stole the 2020 election.

The grand choreography is convoluted: It involves the return of the Jewish people to Jerusalem, the appearance of an Antichrist, some creative timekeeping, and the rapture up to heaven of the faithful, but one of the most important events that these forecasters believed would precede the end of the world was the millennium, or one thousand years of prosperity for God's true believers. People who believe in the millennium and shape their lives around its coming are millenarians. Mormons are technically close to dispensationalist premillennialists, a label we need not dig into here, but I bring it up to show how technical and precisely structured millenarian thinking is, qualities that have helped it seep into other intellectual systems.

Many Mormons once believed that the world would end around 1890, within some believers' lifetimes, giving apocalypse prepping an understandable urgency. When the world kept spinning, the belief that society must be improved or even perfected in preparation for the glorious millennium, whenever it comes, remained. Like many other nineteenth-century millenarians, they originally had a progressive political bent. Mormons were against slavery and alcohol. The social "progress" of nineteenth-century progressives who joined Mormons in these positions was often intertwined with a belief in progress toward the apocalypse.

Even reformers who weren't millenarians adopted aspects of the millenarian mindset: Communists, with their belief in agitating for a catastrophic downfall of the capitalist world to be replaced by a utopic new order, rhymed with their religious peers. And Smith taught his followers that they were to establish a communitarian utopia without private property, distinct from the capitalist Babylon around it.

"I have looked upon the community of Latter-day Saints in vision," Brigham Young taught, "and beheld them organized as one great family of heaven, each person performing his several duties in his line of industry, working for the good of the whole more than for individual aggrandizement; and in this I have beheld the most beautiful order that the mind of man can contemplate."

Initially, this perfected city of Zion, or New Jerusalem, was to be in, of all places, Jackson County, Missouri. If the location seems a little random to you, I don't disagree, but this was the revelation Smith received. Smith led a group there, and they had a good go but were eventually run off by neighbors hostile to Mormons' economic insularity and abolitionism. Mormons generally relied on their own Mormon banks and financial systems and built quite successful settlements on their own. At one point, the Mormon city of Nauvoo, where Smith led his people after Missouri, was the second-largest city in Illinois, behind Chicago. Although early Mormons more or less abandoned the actual site of Zion in Jackson County, Missouri, they took the idea of Zion with them to Utah.

Historian Thomas Carter spent his career studying the folk architecture of the American West and early Mormon architecture in particular. He writes that Brigham Young instructed his followers building out west "not to ravage and despoil the land, but rather to subdue it and make it beautiful." Young specifically mentioned cities, homes, and gardens in his exhortations for followers to create beauty around them. Mormons laid out gridded towns with large lots that were neat and orderly, and aside from the fact that they had temples instead of churches, the settlements were pretty typical of the time for Western American territory. All the unusual religious rituals were hidden away in the temples, where only Mormons could go, so to outsiders, the towns probably seemed pretty normal, if perhaps unusually beautiful. This attractive normality might have helped Mormons recruit followers so successfully, in a way that competing religious sects of the time struggled to do.

It also helped that over the nineteenth century, the church's anti-capitalist ideas softened, bringing it closer to broader American culture. Mormons believe in continuous revelation, meaning church leaders can revise doctrine over time as opposed to sticking inflexibly to old scripture. The firebrand progressivism of the early church cooled, and the new mindset was okay with inequality among the righteous, believing that wealth was proof of God's blessing. Mormons were meant to work hard and improve their community. If God let them be rewarded materially on Earth, then they were doing something right and would continue to be rewarded in heaven. Owning expensive homes, furniture, and clothing meant that a family was living right in God's eyes—there was no reason to hide it.

This embracing of finery mixed with a Zionist mission to create a perfect world distinct from the fallen one around it led to what Carter calls an "aesthetic of artificiality." Early Mormon tastes steered away from log cabins or anything too rustic. Instead, they preferred kiln-fired brick or cut stone buildings that were more refined. More processed materials showed more mastery over the natural environment and the power of Mormon civilization to create perfection and herald the coming of the new world.

As times changed, the aesthetic of artificiality softened but didn't go away.

The nineteenth century progressed, and the borders of Zion weakened. The Transcontinental Railroad linked Utah to the coasts by 1870, and non-Mormons more easily moved into Salt Lake City and other settlements. But the dream of life perfected didn't vanish—Carter writes that the boundaries of Zion shrank from the edges of the region to the individual.

By the end of the nineteenth century, Utah was a state and Mormon society blended more with broader American society. It was a time when Mormons tried to "de-peculiarize" themselves, in the words of art historian Heather Belnap, abandoning polygamy and embracing the American two-party political system. But Mormonism did not disappear. The LDS Church now claims a growing membership of more than 17 million and has temples around the world. Mormons have entered mainstream American society. The Osmond siblings became national stars in the '70s. The Winter Olympics came to Salt Lake City in 2002. Mitt Romney became the 2012 presidential Republican nominee.

The Zionist attitude toward home design has stayed alive. Josh Probert, an expert in the history of Mormon design, has written about Leah Dunford Widtsoe, a 20th-century LDS leader. In an 1899 article, she exhorted Mormon women to take interest in home design to prepare for the world to come. New Jerusalem was to be a city of splendor, where homes would be "luxurious and glorious abodes for eternal spirits."

"Who is to design and build this glorious City of Promise?" Dunford Widtsoe asks. "The faithful Saints of God. Are they preparing themselves for this mighty labor?" Are they improving their current homes in preparation for the work they'll have to do in the future's New Jerusalem?

Today's trad wives and mommy bloggers may not have the construction of New Jerusalem in mind—most of Smith's followers surely don't—and Mormons, for all their success, are still a small minority in the United States and the broader world. Not all home influencers are Saints of God, but a Zionist attitude to worldmaking has been widespread among Americans throughout much of its history, and is still embraced far outside LDS temples.

Anglo-Americans have used Biblical stories to describe their colonial experience since before the country's founding. They underlie the belief in the power of escaping and rebirth. The Puritans, sailing away from England for religious freedom, were following in the footsteps of the Israelites in exodus, or so they thought. Later, during the Second Great Awakening, many Christians became focused on the Jewish people of Israel and getting them to move to the Holy Land as millenarian prophesies envisioned. Mormons were unusual in believing in two Zions, one in America and the other in Palestine; most Christians believed only in the latter. Some focused on the establishment of the modern state of Israel as a step on the road to Jesus's return. Many still support the modern state of Israel for this reason, particularly on the Evangelical Right. Christian Zionism is far from dead.

Mormonism, too, has not just survived but thrived. Two hundred years after its founding, Mormonism is not quite cool, but it and Utah, the religion's global hub, are, in social media parlance, trending. Utah has an unusually high number of reality shows for a state that doesn't even rank among the top twenty-five most populous. Mormon influencer and star of *The Secret Lives of Mormon Wives*, Taylor Frankie Paul, is the lead of the 22nd season of *The Bachelorette*.

Many of Mormonism's values align with the neoliberal era. Carter cites the ideas of the seminal Mormon historian Leonard Arrington about how the religion manages to blend "a Puritan-based corporate work ethic with the strong individualism of Jacksonian democracy." After the LDS Church abandoned its communitarian principles and reduced the borders of Zion to the individual, it created a hustle culture with high stakes: Not only were you to work hard to get ahead in life but also the afterlife, winning God's blessing and preparing your little corner of the world for Christ's return.

The religion also blends well with the neoliberal focus on families. To reach the highest station in the afterlife, celestial heaven, where they can achieve godhood, members must have a celestial marriage, or a union of man and woman for all eternity.

Mormonism ties together a Bachelor's focus on the power of love, a Kardashian's obsession with family, the Real Housewives' existential investment in their homes, *Trading Spaces*'s belief in the power of conversion, an aesthetic of artificiality that would be at home on *Selling Sunset*, a *Fire Island* utopian impulse, and *The Real World*'s embrace of diversity under a white Western tradition. And the church smiles on conspicuous consumption, perfect for any reality star striving to reinvent themself as a social media star.

It's a religion that's made for the influencer era. As Carter points out, the early LDS Church threaded a needle when establishing itself. Like other evangelical religions, it wanted to attract converts, so it had to have a distinctive offering to market. But it couldn't be so different from mainstream Christianity that it would scare people off. "The Mormon landscape became an American landscape of difference, not otherness," Carter writes, "meaning that it became a variation on rather than a departure from the normative tradition." Successful influencers are different but not off-putting. They offer something unusual and worth following but not so unusual that followers stray.

Smith is aspirational but relatable, as any model Mormon should be. This is part of what makes her so successful, even when she's doing what others have already done.

Soon after Smith's videos became famous, another TikToker, Onezwa Mbola, accused Smith of copying her. Mbola makes meals out of items that she's "grown, raised, or foraged," as she announces at the beginnings of her videos, which she narrates in a steady, soothing tone not unlike Smith's. In 2024, Mbola noticed that soon after she posted a video about making boba tea, Smith did the same. Smith denied copying anyone and pointed out that neither TikToker was the first to make boba. Mbola eventually dropped the issue. In a social media world that relies on memes and repeatable formats, defining plagiarism is difficult if not impossible—earlier in the year, some of Smith's followers had accused Mbola of being the one doing the copying. Creators rely on others recreating their dances or imitating their makeup tutorials to get attention and go viral. Algorithms reward new content that resembles existing popular content. Even if

Smith were inspired by Mbola, that would not necessarily run afoul of TikTok morality.

But Mbola's case illustrates the iniquities of the platform. Mbola lives in the South African countryside where she grew up, and her content is arguably a more accurate reflection of how some people really live—aside from the occasional boba-esque diversion, the meals she makes are logical. They're aspirational in their farm-to-table earthiness, but no more so than what you might see in *Bon Appétit*. Throughout 2024, she had fewer than one million followers on TikTok; Smith closed the year with more than 11 million. Mbola's videos focus on the food; her body is barely in frame. She's not a model—she says she has worked in the merchant marines. When she appears in a video showing her fishing, she's in a T-shirt and shorts, nothing remotely like Smith's off-the-runway confections. Mbola has no heartthrob husband to test her creations. She doesn't rage bait and shows her ingredients coming out of the earth; Smith never seems to get her hands dirty, and her creations slide out of her nonstick pans.

Smith embodies the aesthetic of artificiality that the early Mormons pioneered, and audiences love it. There's a world of people online seeking unnatural perfection—it is the missing ingredient in Smith's trad wife–New Domestic–Dimes Square swirl.

In Salt Lake City, I popped into Alpha Coffee, a partly veteran-owned café in the base of a glass-and-steel tower that houses a branch of Goldman Sachs. Alpha Coffee serves drinks such as the Viking, a coffee with butter, honey, and sea salt, and the Spartan, an espresso-based drink with high-protein creamer. The cafe's mission statement is "Awesome Coffee / Be a Warrior / Have Fun / Give Back," and it sells beans online at half price to deployed troops. In the parlance of toxic internet bros, "alphas" are alpha males, supposedly the natural leaders of societies. Alphas exists in a world of content mainly marketed to men that focuses on wellness, masculinity, and optimizing oneself in all areas: professionally, financially, sexually. It's a neoliberal manosphere revolving around what's left after social ties have been blasted away by free market forces: the body. Male influencers advise disciplining it to wake at five A.M. and shocking it with cold plunges, conditioning it with long walks, and supplementing it with injected testosterone and/or coffee with protein. What nature has given is transformed under a man's control.

Salt Lake City was home to Alpha Con, a convention featuring speakers such as Jeremiah "The Bull" Evans, a former BYU football player turned influencer, who posted content about Jesus, meat, and making money. "Be not as you are, but rather as you should be," he captioned a video of him grilling and eating what appear to be two pork chops. Another Instagram posts shows him on a mock *Forbes* magazine cover wearing a suit jacket and a mullet with the headlines "Prioritize financial literacy" and "Push through limitations and realize your capabilities." He has since been sentenced to 96 months in prison for securities fraud and money laundering.

It all seems far from Smith's gentle whispers, but these voices share the aesthetic of artificiality in that they advocate pursuing a world in nature but not of it. Alpha influencers take this pursuit a step further. They advise their followers to buy investment properties and rent them out, the goal being to work smarter, not harder, and earn passive income unlike those boss-following betas. They invest with the logic of finance, stripping homes of cultural ties and seeing them only as assets, flipping houses to cater to real estate appraisal forms. This is the aesthetic of the homes on shows such as *Rock the Block*, the HGTV all-star series in which designers craft houses to have the highest real estate value. It's an aesthetic of capital, perfect for private homes that have no regard for community. These homes, even with all their bells and whistles, are generic, the kind of sellable shell where Smith shot her 2024 viral videos.

This is a world optimized for market efficiency, a collection of personal spheres perfected in preparation for transcendence. It's a selfie Zionism, and it's one of the most powerful forces in the world, shaping what millions want and aspire to.

Millenarianism, despite its promises of destruction, feels good in a world where lonely alienated life feels so bad. Millenarianism gives order to the world. It's not a shellacking, but it assures believers that all this suffering will end with the ultimate makeover. The notion that this apocalyptic timeline is progressing is reassuring. It reframes tragic world events as signs of a greater good to come. It offers the supreme colonial escape: to heaven, where the faithful will eventually go.

Selfie Zionism narrowly focuses not even on believers' homes but on their individual bodies, perfected through complex schemes of calorie counting, workout optimization, and "looksmaxxing," or maximizing physical attractiveness by any means necessary. Selfie Zionism is about presenting an unnaturally constructed self, whether covered with florid gowns, an altered hairline, or steroid-produced muscles. Focusing on oneself is a response not only to neoliberalism blasting away social ties but also of racist fear in societies of diversity. If you don't want to care about other races in a diverse society but don't want to seem racist, you can just care about yourself. It's a way to avoid any scary mixing with others, similar to how Mormons focused on themselves when they were forced to integrate with Gentiles arriving in Utah. And scary others, in turn, have to focus on themselves because no one else is going to.

Work comes home in these selfie Zionist videos, which are ostensibly instructional but are on a different path than HGTV or *Trading Spaces*. These videos are guided by the prosumer fascism of the Kardashians, but now we're not just working at home, we're working *on* our homes and our bodies: cooking, dressing, turning ourselves into projects to be perfected. Our hybrid homes become hybrid bodies, part ours, part property of the ones disciplining us on-screen, forcing us to use every ounce of ourselves to try to feel real, worthy of transcendence to the better place and convincing others to do the same.

Our hybrid selves may soon blend with others that we get to experience or tap into virtually. We'll be able to connect to other experiences while being manipulated and controlled. Cruel homes become cruel selves, hollowed out, the pursuit of feeling real turned into an endless quest.

It's not so easy to avoid this future. Not even some socialist revolution with millenarian overtones could save us. The roots of cruel homes are older than the United States and embody impulses that are not necessarily tied to capitalism, and a turn to communism wouldn't necessarily fix them. But getting all doomsday about the future isn't the ticket, either.

The apocalyptic mindset is contagious. Millenarian thinking, with its ideas about Antichrists and raptures, may seem far-fetched to outsiders, but aspects of it have become pretty normal, at least in certain circles. The spread of doomsday prepping is one example. Mormons have long been avid preppers—early members of the faith often believed that the end of the world would come within their lifetimes. Now it seems that any billionaire worth their bullion has an end-of-the-world compound locked away on some island. The United States' hyper-militarization and military support of the modern state of Israel is partially another example, all gearing up for the prophesied final battle at a place called Armageddon, in Palestine, where blood shall flow as high as a horse's bridle. And rhetoric about a coming climate apocalypse is yet another, one that might have good intentions but might not be engendering the most thoughtful behavior.

The answer is definitely not to aim for perfection in your home or your self or to batten down the hatches while it all goes to pot around you, waiting for some eventual release. Don't buy a home, don't build a home, don't get shredded or bake a trifle while dressed like a pangolin. Don't do anything you think you need to do to feel more real. Avoid being cruel to yourself.

Is the future of the world Utah? No, but if we don't course correct, the future will run though the apocalyptic fantasies that have shaped the state and are shaping our homes, one swipe at a time.

People didn't come here 500 years ago to be friends

Social media hasn't been great for reality TV, and not just because it's outcompeting for eyeballs.

"I feel like social media is the downfall of reality television, because people aren't being real anymore," said former *Real Housewives of Atlanta* producer Carlos King on his *Reality with the King* podcast in July 2024. People on shows have become too concerned about audiences' approval, he thinks. They've become too self-aware and preoccupied with scripting themselves. Some of the genre's old reality effects are becoming less successful.

King is far from the only one with a gloomy outlook on the loss of reality. The previous fall, former star of *The Real Housewives of Atlanta* NeNe Leakes told *The Real Housewives of New York* alum Bethenny Frankel on Frankel's podcast: "I used to be the kinda girl who keeps it one hundred, and now I keep it about seventy-five." Frankel herself had taken to social media instead of returning to reality TV, crowing about how she's now making "direct-to-consumer" content instead of working for entertainment companies' profit.

"It's a bizarre transitional moment," Genevieve Gorder of *Trading Spaces* tells me. "TV's gotten really stagnant and a little boring."

A lot of reality TV now feels like regurgitations of tropes from yesteryear, contestants playing it safe by repeating what's worked in the past to win over fans and hiding anything that may be remotely controversial. It's all started to feel a little uncanny and lifeless, especially compared to what people are doing on social media. TV is out, and TikTok is in because of how much easier it is to just whip out your phone and press record than jump through the hoops required to get a show made on TV, even just a cheap reality one. Sure, the quality of social media content isn't always great, but with so much of it being made, there's more than enough to watch online to make someone forget their Peacock password and instead just scroll for hours.

After decades of competing for audiences' attention, the internet is finally superseding TV not by replacing it with something totally different but by refining what made TV so successful. The internet isn't just beaming moving images directly into private spaces; it's beaming moving images to anywhere our bodies are. Hybrid homes are jumping from TVs to phones, laptops, and other devices, creating even smaller hybrid spaces as they do so. We're moving around not in hybrid cocoons so much as hybrid pens while perfecting our bodies for slaughter.

As times get leaner, the reality TV industry is reacting like the movie industry, recycling content that relies on bankable stars and intellectual property. New shows often recycle old ones by creating crossover environments in which reality stars leave their home franchise and compete or party or do whatever else together. Channels have been doing this with their own stars for years—*The Challenge* has been bringing together alumni from *The Real World* and *Road Rules* on MTV for decades; *Bachelor in Paradise* has been a hub for *Bachelor* and *Bachelorette* castoffs for years. But new hits such as *The Traitors* bring together fan favorites from CBS's *Survivor,* Netflix's *Selling Sunset,* Bravo's *Real Housewives,* and even micro-celebrities from outside reality TV. The third season featured Sam Asghari, best known for being Britney Spears's ex-husband. Distinctions between the worlds behind screens and in front of them continue to blur as the lines between reality TV, social media, and general celebrity disappear.

On their podcast *BFFs*, internet personalities Dave Portnoy, Josh Richards, and Brianna LaPaglia aka Brianna Chickenfry interviewed the Montana Boyz, a group of former Montana Tech football players who found fame on TikTok in 2021 by making videos where they lip-synced to country songs and showed off their muscular bodies against big-sky backdrops in a homoerotic frat boy-meets-rancher closeted Republican senator fantasy kind of way.

Portnoy asks what's next for the guys after their initial viral fame. They don't say much. Chickenfry asks if they can sing. No, they can't sing or dance, says one of the Boyz, Mark Estes, from beneath his black baseball cap. Acting? Chickenfry asks. Portnoy shoots it down. "They're just, like, blockheads, they're Montana blockheads," he says. "They're authentic, which is good." Richards suggests reality TV. Estes says they're thinking about that, for sure. Reality TV is now just another venue to create content that capitalizes on an influencer's appeal.

At the time of that interview, Estes was dating Kristin Cavallari, former star of *The Hills*. Cavallari stepped in when Lauren Conrad left the show, leaving Cavallari to headline with Heidi Montag, who has found a new footing online. Montag and her husband, Spencer Pratt, have become social media stars. In 2024, she went on *Just Trish*, the podcast of YouTuber Trisha Paytas, where Paytas calls her "the Marilyn Monroe of our generation."

"You Snapchat and TikTok all the time," Paytas gushes to Montag. "You guys . . . really are masters at TikTok. Spencer was filming, he was live on TikTok during your birth."

Montag tells Paytas how having "a story arc," such as a birth or another medical procedure, can help make her social media series more popular. “My implants just did really well,” Montag says, referring to her documentation of her breast implant revision surgery.

Reality TV is integrated into the broader spectrum of entertainment, less bizarre or exceptional and just another medium for melodrama and the feeling of reality to ooze into all things. Leakes and other reality stars have reined in the reality of their on-screen behavior so that people will like them more on social media and they can spin off to other shows or brand endorsements or whatever other business. Montag and others are turning social media stories into narrative arcs with hopes of making money and possibly getting larger shows.

Montag was once made to seem like a freak on national television because of her plastic surgeries. Now she has become something of a folk hero. When she and Pratt documented on social media how her house in the Pacific Palisades burned in January 2025 wildfires, fans played her 2010 album, *Superficial*, so much that it sprang to the top of iTunes charts.

“Now, I feel like you guys come across as so lovable, like everyone, like, loves you guys. You guys are, like, the internet mom and dad,” Paytas says. This semi-ironic adoration is far from the genuine disgust Montag elicited when she and Pratt were considered the embodiments of everything wrong with the entertainment industry and the country overall.

“Media keeps changing and evolving,” Montag says. “And it’s nothing you can fight. You just need to change with it and figure out how to thrive and be successful.” She then plugs her and her husband’s crystal company.

“Check out Heidi,” Paytas says in her sign-off. “She’s on TikTok, she’s on Snapchat. She’s literally everywhere.”

“Probably in the street in front of you,” Montag adds, “just hustling everywhere.”

Montag has gone from the entry-level assistant that she was at the start of *The Hills*, glumly staring at her calendar, blocking out an endless nine-to-five, to a very different kind of work, serving personal melodramas to followers, a picture of success in a surreal world, a Christine Quinn–style superhero inspiring the next generation of kids to leave their couches in Poughkeepsie.

Reality TV may be faltering, but the forces splitting people from their physical homes seem to be getting stronger—they're also some of the same forces squeezing reality TV.

If you're a millennial like me or younger, the regulatory root of the problem goes back to the fact that our parents' generations decided in the 1970s, '80s, and '90s that they should take away guardrails that had governed American businesses for decades. Republicans and Democrats alike thought this was a good idea, and for everyone but the very rich, it has turned out to be a horrible one. The decline of reality TV is part of the broader decline of the entertainment industry, which is itself part of the long-term enshittification of just about everything in this country, which is all being bought up by finance executives focused on short-term profits for themselves and nothing else. No legacy building. No rah-rah making America great. Just a bigger beach house for the Blackstone CEO that he can escape to while the world around him burns.

The Great Recession of 2008 made everything worse because the government responded to it not by directly saving working- or middle-class people who were struggling but instead focusing on making it easier for businesses to operate to revive the economy. When the federal reserve brought interest rates down to nearly zero, private equity companies, unrestricted by regulation and empowered by cheap loans, swooped into entertainment, buying companies such as MGM and Miramax. Private equity firms work by collecting money not just to invest in businesses, as investment banks do, but also to buy them. They're a development of the financial deregulation that began in the 1970s, and they are diabolically good at working the angles of this unfettered financial dystopia, often making money even when they drive the companies they've bought to bankruptcy. They put money into new streaming services, which paid off during the COVID pandemic when people were trapped and watching for hours, but when audiences emerged from lockdown and started seeing the sun instead of paying for subscriptions to Peacock and Tubi and whatever else, it was tough times in Hollywood.

It doesn't help that leaders of private equity firms are not good at running businesses. They're successful because they're good at getting other people to give them money and extracting maximum short-term profits from whatever they buy with little regard for what they destroy in the process, whether that be the lives of old people in nursing homes or jobs.

Private equity has not been an easy force to counter partly because it follows the colonial playbook of hiding in unintelligibility. Earlier business goliaths were, at their essence, relatively easy to grasp. Ford makes cars. Apple, computers. Google, a search engine. These are things that people interact with every day, and typically they operate well. Their value is easy to understand. Private equity, however, is not easy to understand.

Consider this description from the *New York Times* of the business activities of Lone Star Funds, one of the firms that bought mortgages from the US government after the 2008 crisis: "The acquisition of distressed mortgages by Lone Star is the engine in a well-oiled securitization machine that assumes that foreclosure and resale of the homes are inevitable components of the process. In these securitizations, many of the soured loans are bundled into bonds that yield up to 4 percent. They are then sold to hedge funds and mutual funds."

The idea of selling a form of debt—a mortgage—is already abstract. Mixing in concepts such as securitization creates a translucent scrim clouding any understanding of the businesses and allowing many activities to hide in the haze.

Technocrats built the private equity era by creating a financial economy that only a select few can fully understand. This is not an environment of free and flexible competition. It's more akin to *America's Next Top Model* or *Project Runway*, which follow rituals of meritocratic competition while producers actually make the decisions about who will win. Private equity is the paragon of the liquid modern era: slippery money, impossible to pin down, sweeping away your world before you have time to know that a new imbecilic finance bro owns it.

As the 2010s progressed, private equity companies helped change the rules of American TV. In the United States, there have been three ages of mass-audience television. The first was the postwar era dominated by the handful of broadcast networks. Then in the '70s and '80s came cable and deregulation, which exploded the number of channels and began the second era of TV, which ended with the rise of a new outlet: streaming services, or streamers. These are companies such as Netflix that stream videos on demand to audiences via the internet—entertainment on demand.

Streaming was supposed to be the great new third age of TV. It's perfect for the new gig economy, under which the strictures of the standard nine-to-five labor schedule are gone, along with guaranteed pensions or health insurance. "Flexible labor, flexible leisure," writes Anna Kornbluh about the age of streamers in *Immediacy: Or, The Style of Too Late Capitalism*. When people are hustling to survive, they can't sit down for appointment viewing. They have to stream when they can.

Private equity pumped money into streaming, but now social media is taking the spot that streaming had, and the private equity money is drying up. Historian Daniel Bessner has estimated that the TV industry cut more than a quarter of its jobs between August 2022 and the end of 2023. Los Angeles could become the new Detroit, ravaged by a once-dominant American industry that falters and moves abroad.

Private equity is mucking up housing, too.

"In 2011, no landlord in America owned more than a thousand single-family home rental properties," reports federal prosecutor Brendan Ballou in *Plunder: Private Equity's Plan to Pillage America.* "By 2013 . . . Blackstone bought more than that in a single day."

In the post–mortgage crisis era, private equity firms emerged as the government's "heroes" to save the housing system, taking over where lenders had so spectacularly failed by buying foreclosed homes. But private equity firms aren't known to share their wealth. Private equity firms have bought clusters of homes, getting inordinate power in certain markets by dominating local housing supply. They haven't resold many of the homes they've bought but have instead rented them out and piled fees on the new tenants. Often, they've targeted poor people because they have less ability to take their money elsewhere when their new landlords cut back on maintenance and load them with fees. Atlanta is perhaps the hardest hit city. In some of its suburbs, private equity companies own the majority of single-family rentals.

Now, companies like Blackstone own millions of homes in the U.S. and are major investors in entertainment and news companies, renting reality to people who increasingly can't afford it. Virtual surreality is here. We don't have to put on headsets. It's what social media, news, the rental market, and reality TV create, working together to get people to consume the feeling of being real. The long-term outlook isn't great. Our digital-physical hybrid homes are owned by people with a five-year investment return timeline.

These are investors who care only about making money for themselves, selfie Zionists with no agenda other than maximizing their net worth, enabled by the same deregulation behind hustle culture, the gig economy, and life without a safety net. These are believers in a rugged individualism obsessed with leaving society behind and finding a new life for yourself out on the prairie or in a suburban mansion in the hills, safely removed from the needy masses. It's the long arc of Western history, bending toward an abstract and impersonal system of justice based on a faith in the power of the individual disconnected from the people around them or the land they're on. Now, any connections to land or people are being sold back to you—it's the dynamic that makes life feel less real and is so cruelly disappointing. No market force is really interested in reconnecting you to your land or people. If you did reconnect, then you wouldn't need the middleman anymore. Instead we've become dependent on and emotionally invested in convoluted systems of private property and media environments that make life so precariously surreal.

It all just feels wrong. This general dysphoria is hard to exactly characterize because it's so foundational to our ways of living. And it's only going to get worse as the world gets more liquid and these cruel scripts get embedded in the technology shaping our lives.

But it doesn't have to be this way.

In *Building the Dream: A Social History of Housing in America*, architectural historian Gwendolyn Wright writes about how strange apartment living seemed to many 19th-century Americans. It was a suspect, foreign thing. Okay in freaky-deaky Paris, but in this country? No. People were supposed to live in their own homes, their own buildings. Strangers living together was unwholesome. Who knew what could happen? People fretted about potential promiscuity between families living on the same floor and associated any apartment building with overcrowded tenements. The moral panic continued even after apartment living had caught on in American cities. Wright quotes a 1917 critic: "Sex morality often is by subtle ways weakened through long-established apartment house living." As late as the 1920s, the

Ladies' Home Journal warned of a Bolshevik influence on American women via apartments.

In one hundred years, what now-strange way of living could seem normal?

"I dream of the day that there's a woman on television, full stop, let alone on *The Housewives*, who's like, You know what? I rent. I'm proud to rent," Adrienne Brown tells me. It would be a sign that the obsession with homeownership might be slipping. But she points out that people have deep emotional ties to the idea of homeownership, even Black families who may know on some level that the system is not set up for them to succeed. "That kind of affective trap around homeownership is really hard to break out of, and for really real reasons . . . you can't just be like, you know, your grandmother who really believed in homeownership and like, put all of her life savings into the home—you know what? Maybe she was wrong. No one wants to hear that."

Change is hard, especially when we're changing centuries of accumulated problems that people have invested in for generations. It's pretty clear that the state of housing in this country is abysmal—homes are unaffordable, isolating, and environmentally destructive, shaped by aesthetics of colonial amnesia and cold white LED artificiality; the latent suffering of suburbia is turning acute and crying out for change; leaders are turning rage-baiting ideas into reality; racism abounds—but it's less clear what to do about it. Part of the system's cruelty is that it keeps you thinking that if only you invest in it further, it'll finally pay off.

Lackluster solutions abound: Techno-optimists offer ideas such as 3D-printed or factory-made homes that don't address deeper political issues. Pro-developer YIMBYs cheer on housing construction, usually to a landlord's benefit. Wonks twist the knobs of public policy as though solving the country's housing issues were a matter of tuning to the right frequency on the radio. Tiny home builders dream of providing people with the bare minimum to survive. The government's got its HOPE. But these notions aren't addressing the fundamental issues with housing in this country—the assumption that everyone should be living with a nuclear family, that homeownership is essential to humanity, that buildings should try to tame nature instead of coexisting with it, that the land belongs to people who stole it and the systems they created to despoil it.

There are some basic things, such as tenant protections, rent stabilization, and investment in public housing, that would help in the short term, but hybrid homes are monsters more complex than can be addressed by these relatively simple solutions. We need to radically rethink our ideas of home and connection to avoid ending up in a situation where the feeling of reality is a luxury that we have to buy from some private equity gorgon.

People have tried. In *Redesigning the American Dream,* historian Dolores Hayden documents the work of nineteenth-century material feminists such as Melusina Fay Peirce who envisioned cooperative neighborhoods with community kitchens and laundries to liberate Victorian women from being sequestered in private homes, doing housework all day for no pay. In *The Residential is Racial,* Brown writes about author Richard Wright's photo essay *12 Million Black Voices,* in which he envisions Black American families supported not by the "ideals of the Lords of the Land" but "love, sympathy, pity and the goading knowledge that we must work together to make a crop."

In the 1960s, civil rights activists, along with Southern Black farmers, created the first community land trust. That model shares land ownership across a cooperative community and has been gathering momentum slowly since. Ideally, this kind of shared ownership is not just a financial system but a way of encouraging people to be more invested in each other's welfare more generally.

These models recognize that the problem is not just that housing is unaffordable. They acknowledge that homes structure how people relate to each other and their environs and that people have to rethink their relations before anything will really improve.

Designers have also recognized that the architectural style of a home matters, too. Style can shape how people think about their homes, what kinds of behaviors and activities they accommodate, how they announce who belongs and who doesn't. Bachelor Mansion–esque nostalgia isn't the answer, and neither is making architecture more "modern," as Christine Quinn and Fire Island have shown, but there are alternatives.

Architects like Joseph Martinez have theorized a Chicanx style of architecture associated with the Chicano civil rights movement, when urban infrastructure built to clear Mexican-American neighborhoods was adapted by communities and artists to serve the people it was meant to break. Chicano Movement designers didn't deny a colonial past or pursue some fantasy of starting over from a tabula rasa but dealt with what had been built and reworked it, similar to Kyle Carrero Lopez's vision of dystopia queered. Different styles of architecture create homes for different cultures, and the country needs many more styles than ones developed by and for Anglo settlers.

But the trajectory of cruel homes started a long time ago, and deep, old impulses guide them. Our current deregulated economy may be a relatively new development, but it's a development of ancient plans. In our liquid modern world, these old cruel forces have more flexibility to shape our experiences, to penetrate deeper into ourselves, stealing more and more from us.

There is one linchpin tying this mess together, a knot that Saint Augustine and all that were leading up to and from which our generalized dysphoria dangles: the fact that the land most American homes are built on is stolen.

"Many centuries ago, Saint Augustine, a saint of my church, wrote that a people was a multitude defined by the common objects of their love," said Joe Biden in his presidential inaugural address. "What are the common objects we as Americans love? That define us as Americans?" He listed some—"opportunity, security, liberty" among them—before ending with "the truth." He made these remarks two weeks after rioters stormed the Capitol, believing the election had been stolen from Donald Trump. "There is truth and there are lies," Biden said. "Lies told for power and for profit. And each of us has a duty and responsibility . . . to defend the truth and defeat the lies."

If there's one word that doesn't have much to do with how Americans live, it is "truth." People in this country live in fantasy worlds. Lies told for power and for profit have shaped the ways pretty much everyone in this country lives. People have lied that single-family homes are more virtuous than apartments, that Black people are bad homeowners, that farming is easy, that competitive isolation is the way to go, that the land this country is built on belongs to European colonizers who swindled Native peoples and broke the treaties they made whenever they felt like it. So many commentators have warned that the Trump presidencies have been steps toward fascism, but political fascism is something that happened 100 years ago in Europe. We have our own distinct flavor of cruelty.

Worrying about the loss of American democracy is just another kind of nostalgia for the country's more individualistic colonial past. Stop trying to recreate a myth that we're a bunch of yeoman farmers working together to turn wilderness into a democratic Zion. Start seeing those farms as colonial settlements that have taken other people's land. Chuck the whole thing out. Embrace better ways of living with each other and the land.

Americans don't need to worry about sliding into dystopia. Americans are already living in the dystopia other societies have warned each other about, the one that steals people's land and erases their culture while telling them that they're just helping out—genocide G. I. Joe, smiling while he destroys everything you've ever known. The threat of fascism makes the status quo seem better, though, which works great for people thriving in this broken system. Private equity billionaires don't need fascism. They're already doing great. But they need the threat of fascism so that people continue to defend the system as it is.

"We're not in a post-colonial society," writes activist and scholar Taiaiake Alfred in his book *It's All About the Land*. "We're in a contemporary colonial society."

Colonialism isn't an original sin or Freudian trauma needing healing—it's how we're living now. It's written into homes across the country. I grew up, like millions of others, in a Colonial Revival–style home, one with white vinyl siding and red plastic shutters. Other people live in Spanish Colonial Revival–style homes, still others in homes that harken back to plantations or ranches on the Western frontier. It's not like a colonial mindset is deeply hidden; it's just mundane enough to be invisible, at least to the people who benefit from it.

Unfortunately, as obvious as the subpar state of things may be when you really start looking, undoing colonial society is not so easy. You would have to disentangle dense webs of inscrutable liquid modern policies run by condescending technocrats who smugly shake their heads and say "You don't understand, it's complicated" to anyone who contradicts them. But as Kristin T. Ruppel put it to me: "Humans created this. Humans should be able to figure it out."

The thing is, I don't think anyone is particularly happy with this situation, not even the people on top. There's a certain strange dysphoria that comes from being unable to accept reality, and most Americans are unwilling to accept their reality: that they are occupiers living on occupied land.

"I didn't come here to make friends," countless cutthroat reality TV stars have told their audiences and competitors, and Alfred, presumably unintentionally, echoes them: "People didn't come here 500 years ago to be friends," he writes about Canada. "They came to escape their own lives in other parts of the world and to exploit."

That's not exactly a recipe for long-lasting happiness.

Centuries later, we still see people dreaming of existential makeovers, hoping that the next reveal will show a portrait of success. In *Redesigning the American Dream*, Hayden quotes Henry James writing in 1904 in the voice of New Jersey suburban villas in "The American Scene": "We are only instalments, symbols, stop-gaps . . . we have nothing to do with continuity, responsibility, transmission, and don't in the least care what becomes of us after we have served our present purpose."

In this slippery, surreal private-equity age, this kind of short-term thinking has gotten even shorter. Forget generational planning—our economic overlords aren't even planning for the next ten years. No wonder even billionaires like the Kardashian-Jenners are living in houses designed by fear. Half the country is burning and the other half is sliding into the sea because it's controlled by people who came here to extract what they could, wipe out the people who knew how to live in harmony with the land, and build some simulation of a private heaven while waiting for the world to end.

Even people who aren't occupiers or who are descendants of people brought here unwillingly are being sucked into a living situation driven by competition and soulless economic formulas. The most naive homebuyer now has to compete with financial professionals who consider homes to be abstract assets, no different from the newspapers or nursing homes they're buying, gutting, and flipping for a quick buck. The spirit of competition pervades, but it's not competition on equal terms. Fortune favors the rich, unencumbered by emotional attachments or moral prerogatives to do good. And everyone is left trying to fill an emotional hole with fantasies of feeling real. The cruelty.

The feeling of reality has become a luxury, and this chapter of history may be remembered as the era of searching for realness. This drive has taken advantage of regulatory and technological changes to create what we call reality TV, and it will continue to shape how we use new technologies and media even if we ditch the genre, unless we are able to move in a radically different direction.

Vine Deloria Jr. wrote about the split between people and nature at the heart of colonial societies. We probably have to do something about that if we're going to pivot.

It's all about the land, Alfred reminds readers.

Home is more than just shelter or a commodity built on a lot. "There's reciprocity: the plants, the animals, the natural environment, give something to us, we give something to them," Alfred writes about Indigenous relationships with land.

He also writes that in order to solve the problems of colonization, we must "put Indigenous people back on the land." Decolonizing should not just be designing for diversity but actually giving land back. Not only is it the just thing to do, but it's better for everyone. It would help everyone avoid the habit of white people trying to live more "real" lives by emulating Native Americans or Mexicans or whoever else. And it would help avoid the failures of well-intentioned liberals of the past, like the progressive peers of Helen Hunt Jackson, who presumed to solve problems for Native Americans and instead made more.

The idea is not that Native Americans will magically save the day but that ways of living that are designed in concert with the land with millennia of experience, ones that have a goal of maintaining landscapes and ecosystems, will do better than whatever transcendental fantasies of progress have done for the past 500 years. The goal is not a diverse society under white rule or some kind of rainbow colonialism but a shift away from the direction that white people have pushed this part of the world. Restoring land to Indigenous peoples is a step toward remedying the web of problems that colonialism has created. The process need not be violent and destructive—that would be the colonizer way. It could be as joyful and productive as the growing Land Back movement already is.

Apartment living was shocking a century ago and is now normal. Restored Indigenous land could be just as common in another one hundred years. The United States has had an okay run at best. Colonialism, it turns out, doesn't feel very good, even for the colonizers. Why not try something different?

I wrote a lot of this book during the January 2025 Los Angeles fires, watching videos on social media of military jets dumping fire retardant while burning through fossil fuels to save neighborhoods built on fantasies of white utopias. People are raising money for recovery on social media, a symptom of a system where only people with marketable personalities can win support. My friends are sending me weird AI-generated videos that probably required as much electricity as a small apartment building to create, only to be double-tapped by audiences primed to desire an aesthetic of artificiality. I've spent months watching news reels that show American-made weapons flattening homes in Palestine as they have done for decades around the world. Trump has been up to God knows what since the time I finished writing this. Americans pretend they're in heaven as they turn Earth into hell.

We don't need more cruel homes or surreal melodramas making us feel better off than we are. We need ways of living that feel good, not just in the moment or in a five-year profit timeline or a five-episode arc, but over lifetimes and generations. We need to live with reality and not just consume things that give the feeling of it. The land is solid, and it's where we can build an alternative to a liquid modern world.

There's reason for grounded optimism. Brown points out how a housing system as broken as ours may force people to try out new things: "If you're not able to buy your first home until thirty-five or forty, you learn how to be attached to places in different ways." People are developing new habits whether they want to or not.

What reality TV homes show us is how much we yearn to feel real. It's strange that any society could succeed while taking away that simple feeling, so basic to existence, and selling (or renting) it back to us. We don't need to rehabilitate reality TV; we need a new relationship to our reality in general, one unmediated by Kris Jenner or Andy Cohen or even Heidi Montag. Hybrid spaces are probably here to stay. But we need not detach ourselves from the physical world around us and stare at our screens in hopes of ascending to a more perfect realm. Salvation won't be found in the grids of a perfect city or a pixelated screen. There are other paths.

ACKNOWLEDGMENTS

This book wouldn't exist without my agent Danielle Bukowski and my editors at Astra: Deborah Ghim, who first believed in it, and Tara Sharma, who guided it into being and expertly improved it. This book also relies on the talented work of everyone involved in the publication process: managing editor Jane Handa, copyeditor Dan O'Connor, proofreader Alison Cherry, interior designer Alissa Theodor, in-house designer Frankie DiGiovanni, cover designers Rodrigo Corral Studio and Giacomo Girardi, senior publicist Alexis Nowicki, senior marketing manager Tiffany Gonzalez, and Emily Bell, editorial director at Astra.

Laurie Ouellette's essays and books on the history of reality TV provided the foundation for this book, along with the analytical approaches of Sianne Ngai, Lauren Berlant, Vine Deloria Jr., and my undergraduate advisor, John Stilgoe. Ngai's positive feedback was also a massive dose of encouragement that has helped sustain me through the publication process. The New York Public Library, and its research collection, particularly the Art and Architecture Collection, also helped sustain my writing process by giving me a physical place to work and an invaluable resource for my research. Ruth McCormick at the Riverside Public Library also helped me in a pinch when I thought there was no way I was going to find a certain bit of information.

This book also relied on extensive interviews. Thank you to everyone who gave their time and thoughts: Robin Aranza, Michelle Aulisio, Laura Barraclough, Adrienne Bown, Mark Bullivant, Tony Campbell, Bob D'Antonio, Jennifer Davidson, Paige Davis, George De La Nuez, Tariq Dixon, Akira Drake Rodriguez, Danielle Faraldo, Doug Fregolle,

Tomer Fridman, Genevieve Gorder, Brian Graden, Dianne Harris, Jed Holtz, James Jacobs, Aaron Johnson, Matt Keegan, Alex Keomurjian, Josh Koral, Rosalind Krauss, Ryan Levis, Amelia Modlin, Isabelle Morley, Patricia Morton, Tarisai Ngangura, Jason Oppenheim, Joseph Pell Lombardi, Ty Pennington, Jhoiey Ramirez, Christopher Rawlins, Kristin Ruppel, Angelic Rutherford, Tara Sandler, Edwina Sandys, Leigh Seaman, Laurie Smith, Julie Tarr, Nick Thompson, Lauren Weiss Bricker, Doug Wilson, and Kristina Wilson.

Thank you also to John Trujillo for helping with research, and my colleagues at *Dwell*, who edited the essays that became chapters of this book and talked through ideas: Bill Hanley, Kate Dries, Ian Zunt, Alana Levinson, Don Armstrong, Meredith Clark, and Will Allstetter. Special thanks to my big sister in book writing, TV watching, and general dissatisfaction, Megan Reynolds, who made the most annoying days a little more manageable and continues to guide my way through the media world. Thank you also to friends who talked through my harebrained ideas and provided better ones along with loads of encouragement, and/or just sent me many texts about bad TV: Regina Bediako, Alex Chabla, Ed Hsu, Tal Liu, Henry Ng, Melissa Shin, Marielle Woods, Mei Lun Xue, and especially Sascha Feldman, this book's biggest cheerleader. A special thank you to Adam Jasienski's friendship and feedback, which helped me believe that I could actually finish a book like this. Over the years, my writing group partners, Becky Chang, Ariel Davis, and Chris Lorraine, helped me learn to string words together, and finally, my family has supported me while I have strung the years together. Thank you to them most of all.

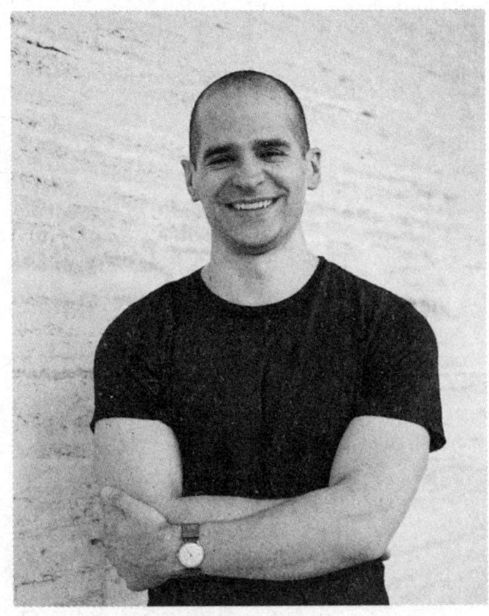

Erin Kim

ABOUT THE AUTHOR

Jack Balderrama Morley is a former/recovering architectural designer and is now the managing editor at *Dwell.* Their writing has appeared in *The New Yorker, Dwell,* and *The Architect's Newspaper,* among other places.